Pamela Oberhuemer • Inge Schreyer
Workforce Profiles in Early Childhood
Education and Care

Pamela Oberhuemer
Inge Schreyer

Workforce Profiles in Early Childhood Education and Care

Trends and Challenges
in 33 European Countries

Verlag Barbara Budrich
Opladen • Berlin • Toronto 2025

All rights reserved. No part of this publication may be reproduced, stored in or introduced into a retrieval system, or transmitted, in any form, or by any means (electronic, mechanical, photocopying, recording or otherwise) without the prior written permission of Verlag Barbara Budrich. Any person who does any unauthorized act in relation to this publication may be liable to criminal prosecution and civil claims for damages. You must not circulate this book in any other binding or cover and you must impose this same condition on any acquirer.

A CIP catalogue record for this book is available from Die Deutsche Nationalbibliothek (The German National Library): https://portal.dnb.de.

Funded by:

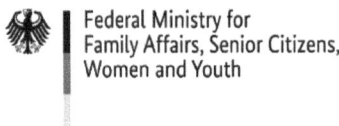

Federal Ministry for
Family Affairs, Senior Citizens,
Women and Youth

Carbon compensated production
© 2025 by Verlag Barbara Budrich GmbH, Opladen, Berlin & Toronto
www.budrich.eu

    ISBN 978-3-8474-3071-1 (Paperback)
    eISBN 978-3-8474-3205-0 (PDF)
    DOI   10.3224/84743071

Verlag Barbara Budrich GmbH
Stauffenbergstr. 7. D-51379 Leverkusen Opladen, Germany
86 Delma Drive. Toronto, ON M8W 4P6 Canada
www.budrich.eu

Cover design by Bettina Lehfeldt, Kleinmachnow – www.lehfeldtgraphic.de
Printed in Europe on FSC®-certified paper by Libri Plureos, Hamburg

Preface and acknowledgments

This book presents summarised findings from a study on the staff working with young children in early childhood education and care (ECEC) settings in 33 countries across Europe.[1] It marks the conclusion of the SEEPRO-3[2] study, the fourth in a series of research projects spanning a period of 30 years, all based at the State Institute for Early Childhood Research and Media Literacy in Munich and funded by the German Federal Ministry for Family Affairs, Senior Citizens, Women and Youth.

The focus is on the core practitioners, centre leaders and co-working staff in the 27 member states of the European Union and in six non-EU countries: *Austria, Belgium, Bulgaria, Croatia, Cyprus, Czech Republic, Denmark, Estonia, Finland, France, Germany, Greece, Hungary, Ireland, Italy, Latvia, Lithuania, Luxembourg, Malta, The Netherlands, Norway, Poland, Portugal, Romania, Russia, Serbia, Slovakia, Slovenia, Spain, Sweden, Switzerland, Ukraine, United Kingdom.*

Comprehensive ECEC Workforce Profiles written by specialists in each of these countries according to a detailed research specification provided by the SEEPRO researchers, together with a synopsis of background Key Contextual Data on the 33 ECEC systems, are presented on a designated webpage. These reports and system profiles in English and German (approx. 4,000 pages in all) form the basis for this book, which also appears in German. They provide in-depth information and analyses on the topics covered here. This book should therefore be understood as a complementary publication to the SEEPRO website (https://www.seepro.eu), where all further country-specific details can be found.

The research team could not have conducted this study without the expertise and cooperative approach of the 50 early childhood experts – most of them academics and researchers, but also policy analysts and ministry officials – in the 33 participating countries. Without the country-specific knowledge of these partners, we would not be in a position to present these findings to a wider audience. Their names and affiliations are included at the end of this book.

Our sincere thanks go to them all and also to colleagues in Germany, England and beyond who have been supportive over the years. Any factual errors in this book publication and any views expressed are the sole responsibility of the authors.

Pamela Oberhuemer, Inge Schreyer
Munich, August 2024

---

1 Project duration: March 2021 to February 2024, ZMV I 7-2515081088.
2 The acronym SEEPRO stands for Systems of Early Education and Professionalisation in Europe.

Contents

Preface and acknowledgments 5

Introduction to SEEPRO-3 11
    SEEPRO-3 – project with a history 11
    SEEPRO-3 – background, aims and procedures 12

Part I
Contextualising the ECEC workforce 15

1   Conceptual framework – a 'science of difference' 17

2   Three ECEC system types: unitary, part-integrated, bi-sectoral 19

3   Key policy measures since the previous SEEPRO study 23
    3.1   Legislative changes 23
    3.2   Curricular reforms 26
    3.3   Measures to improve access to ECEC 28
    3.4   Personnel-related measures 29

4   Contextual Framework 31
    4.1   Legal entitlement and compulsory enrolment in ECEC 31
    4.2   ECEC providers and main setting types 39
    4.3   Curricular frameworks – digital education 42
    4.4   Evaluation and assessment 46
    4.5   Inclusion and transitions 50

    4.6   Working parents, parenting leave and post-leave entitlement to ECEC 53

Part II
The ECEC workforce 57

5   Key pedagogical and specialist support staff 59
    5.1   Core practitioners: minimum qualification requirements and professional profiles 59
    5.2   Centre leaders in ECEC 67
    5.3   Assistant co-workers 73
    5.4   ECEC counsellors, supervisors and inspectors 76
    5.5   Specialist support staff 80
    5.6   Staff in ECEC settings by qualification and gender: an overview 82

6   Initial professional education of core practitioners 85
    6.1   What competences do ECEC core practitioners need? Competence profiles in six countries 85
    6.2   Curriculum in ECEC initial professional education: Six country examples 93
    6.3   Field practice in the initial professional education of ECEC core practitioners 100

7   Alternative routes into the ECEC professions – lateral entry 105

8   Continuing professional development in the early childhood field 109
    8.1   Legislation and regulatory frameworks 109
    8.2   Providers and main forms of continuing professional development 110
    8.3   Continuing professional development as an entitlement and a duty 111
    8.4   Participation in continuing professional development measures as a requirement for career promotion 112

	8.5	Current topics in CPD 113
	8.6	Availability of continuing professional development for ECEC assistant co-workers 114

9 Newly qualified and newly appointed staff: Support measures in the workplace 115

Part III
Reform initiatives – workforce and ECEC system challenges 117

10 Staff-related policy initiatives and reform strategies 119
    10.1 Initiatives to improve initial professional education 119
    10.2 Strategies to improve working conditions and measures to combat staff shortages 120
    10.3 Staff-related reforms as part of overall educational policy strategies 121

11 Staff-related and system-related challenges from a country expert perspective 123
    11.1 Staff shortages 123
    11.2 Staff to child ratios 123
    11.3 Initial professional education of core practitioners 124
    11.4 Continuing professional development opportunities for centre leaders, core practitioners and assistant co-workers 125
    11.5 Integration at the ECEC system level 125
    11.6 Equitable access to early childhood education and care settings 126
    11.7 Further challenges from a country expert perspective 126

12 Summary and outlook 129
    12.1 Contextual framework 129
    12.2 Early childhood staff 131
    12.3 Reform strategies – staff and system-related challenges 132
    12.4 Outlook 134

References 135

About the authors 147

SEEPRO-3 Cooperation partners in 33 countries (2021–2024) 149

Glossary 151

Index 153

Introduction to SEEPRO-3

SEEPRO-3 – project with a history

Since the mid-1990s, four intermittent research projects at the State Institute for Early Childhood Research and Media Literacy (IFP) have focused specifically on the staff working in early childhood education and care settings in Europe. All four projects were funded by the German Federal Ministry for Family Affairs, Senior Citizens, Women and Youth. Following the Maastricht Treaty in 1992, the founding of the European Union and the onset of subsequent strategies to promote the mobility of skilled workers throughout Europe, it also became essential in the early childhood field to know what kind of initial professional education ECEC staff in other countries, who might look for work in Germany, had experienced.

Over this period of 30 years, there has been a steadily growing interest throughout Europe in the governance structures in the field and the country-specific qualification requirements for staff working in ECEC. The four projects have progressively expanded in terms of the number of participating countries and the research questions addressed to early childhood experts in different national contexts. From the outset, a key approach of these studies has been to present data on the workforce in the context of the respective national system of early childhood education and care. All major findings have been published in both English and German.

The *first study* (Oberhuemer/Ulich 1997) focused on the workforce and ECEC systems in the 15 European Union countries of that time: *Austria, Belgium, Denmark, Finland, France, Germany, Greece, Ireland, Italy, Luxembourg, The Netherlands, Portugal, Spain, Sweden* and the *United Kingdom*. Alongside commissioning reports from researchers in the field, key informants were interviewed during five-day visits to each country: representatives of relevant ministries, researchers, teacher educators, ECEC counsellors and professional development experts, representatives of professional organisations and unions as well as staff working in early childhood centres.

This interview-based approach was continued in the *second study*, the first to use the acronym SEEPRO. Including the new central and eastern European Union member states (*Bulgaria, Czech Republic, Estonia, Hungary, Latvia, Lithuania, Poland, Romania, Slovakia* and *Slovenia*) as well as *Cyprus* and *Malta* in southern Europe, the workforce in 27 countries was now in focus and the findings published in book form (Oberhuemer/Schreyer/Neuman 2010).

In 2015, a *third study* was commissioned to address the growing policy priorities in ECEC in Germany and across Europe and to update and extend the existing workforce profiles. By this time, *Croatia*, where a five-day research visit was carried out, had become a new EU member state. Russia and Ukraine were also included in this new round of country reviews since at that time, teachers from these two countries – also early childhood teachers – were increasingly seeking employment in Germany, where only scant information was available for policy administrations about the kind of professional education/training they had received. For the first time, 30 country reports with background data were published on a specially designated website and made accessible (https://www.seepro.eu), free of charge, to all interested readers across Europe and beyond (Oberhuemer/Schreyer 2018).

The SEEPRO-3 study is the *fourth study* in this series of research projects. Knowledge sharing is reaching an ever higher level, with numerous cross-national reports and recommendations on ECEC appearing after the seminal work of the European Commission Network on Childcare (1996) and the first two Starting Strong studies of the OECD (2001, 2006).[3] Nevertheless, the SEEPRO studies remain unique in this landscape in that they provide in-depth country-specific reports on the ECEC workforce by national experts according to a detailed research specification which are backed up by key contextual data of the respective ECEC systems.

SEEPRO-3 – background, aims and procedures

Throughout Europe, early childhood education and care systems are subject to constant shifts, undergoing both expansion and consolidation. Following the growing prioritisation of ECEC in many countries, a landscape of reform strategies and innovations is emerging. The staff working in ECEC settings are recognised as the key contributing factor towards ensuring sensitive interactions with young children, enhancing their individual and group wellbeing and providing a stimulating environment for exploration and learning. At the same time, reform initiatives are hindered by a – in some cases severe – shortage of qualified staff in almost all countries (see also European Commission 2023). This has brought – perhaps more than ever before – the qualification, competence and task profiles of early childhood leaders, pedagogues and assistant co-workers to the forefront of professional policy interest and makes it necessary to continuously update the available data.

Through a comprehensive review and mapping approach, SEEPRO-3 aims to compile a detailed picture of the ECEC workforce across Europe, drawing on both qualitative and quantitative data and analysis relating to 33 countries.

---

3 These include the following: Council of the European Union 2019, 2022; European Commission 2014, 2018, 2021; European Commission/EACEA/Eurydice 2019a, b; 2023.

The research specification for the experts commissioned to write an ECEC Workforce Profile, mostly long-standing cooperation partners, included questions on the following ten aspects:

1. ECEC governance
2. Staffing profile: regular contact staff in ECEC settings; centre leaders; centre-based posts of responsibility; coordinating and supervisory staff; specialist support staff
3. Structural composition of ECEC workforce: qualifications, gender, ethnicity
4. Initial professional education (IPE); initial qualifying routes – higher education and vocational; competences, curriculum and pedagogic-didactic approaches in IPE programmes; alternative entry and qualification routes, system permeability
5. Guided workplace experience (field practice) in the initial professional education of core practitioners
6. Continuing professional development (CPD) opportunities
7. Working conditions and current workforce issues: remuneration; full-time and part-time employment; support measures in the workplace for newly qualified and newly appointed staff; non-contact time; current staffing issues (e.g. staff shortages, recruitment strategies, age distribution)
8. Recent policy reforms and initiatives relating to staffing and professionalisation issues
9. Recent country-specific research focusing on ECEC staff
10. Workforce challenges – country expert assessment.

For each of the 33 countries in the SEEPRO-3 study, two documents have been compiled:

– An *ECEC workforce profile*, i.e. a report based on the above ten criteria. The final versions are the product of a long period of close and continuous clarification and collaboration between the editors and the authors. The reports vary in length, depending on the specific conditions in the respective country. They are also published online in a complete edition with an ISBN for easier citation.
– A key contextual data synopsis draws together *country-specific background information* on the main features of the ECEC system and also relevant demographic data. These were compiled by the project team and reviewed, validated and in some cases co-authored by the cooperation partners.

All documents are available in English and in German on the SEEPRO-3 website (https://www.seepro.eu), thus providing an easily accessible resource for a wide audience across Europe and beyond: early childhood teacher educators in higher and vocational education, national and local government administrations, employers and service providers in the ECEC field, researchers, early childhood staff and other interested persons.

Part I

Contextualising the ECEC workforce

1 Conceptual framework – a 'science of difference'

What do we mean by 'comparing' the ECEC workforce across the SEEPRO-3 countries? Persons with a lived experience of even just two different ECEC systems realise that a one-on-one comparison is impossible, too diverse are the underlying images of children and learning and assumptions about what constitutes a 'good education' during the years leading up to primary school. Our approach was guided by the involvement of one of the authors in the first two Starting Strong reviews of the OECD (2001, 2006), with their richly contextualised backgrounds.

The Portuguese comparative education scholar, Antonio Nóvoa (2018), distinguishes between a 'science of difference' and a 'science of solution'. Diana Sousa and Peter Moss (2022: 402) draw on these two concepts to argue that "…respecting and valuing diversity discourages solutionist technocratic comparative education approaches." This respect for diversity, this 'science of difference', fits best with our understanding and approach. SEEPRO-3 is not a solution-finding study, more a contextualisation of difference. Disregarding the context could lead to a ranking of countries, which is certainly not our intention. A 'science of difference' acknowledges the complexity of ECEC ecosystems (see also Kagan/Roth 2017). Whether and how the enactment of national policies takes place depends on a plethora of forms and diverse interrelationships and networks at the regional/local policy and praxis levels.

Within this conceptual framework, a specific focus on the staff working in ECEC settings, on professional profiles and staffing structures across countries, implies acknowledging that conceptualisations of the ECEC workforce, of the knowledge and skills required, of the support that staff need and the working conditions they experience, are situated and context-specific. They are located in ECEC systems with differing underpinning cultural beliefs and values. They are not only deeply rooted in country-specific histories of ECEC but also intricately linked to socio-political, philosophical and ethical policy stances.

An awareness of these differences is more likely to spark off a line of thinking which challenges one's own images and taken-for-granted assumptions regarding the staff in ECEC and the systems they work in, potentially opening the way for future-oriented innovations.

2 Three ECEC system types: unitary, part-integrated, bi-sectoral

The kind of ECEC system that early childhood professionals find themselves in varies considerably across countries and inevitably influences the way that they view themselves as professionals and how they understand and interpret their professional role. The structure of these systems has been described as being on a continuum between 'integrated' and 'split' in terms of the consistency and coherence of ECEC policies (European Commission/EACEA/Eurydice 2019a; 2019b: 14).

In the SEEPRO-3 study we have chosen three categories to describe the 33 ECEC systems: *unitary, part-integrated, bi-sectoral*. Five criteria are used to distinguish between them.

Table 1 gives an overview of the countries that we have classified as a *unitary* ECEC system, where there is ONE lead ministry, ONE legal framework, ONE curricular framework, ONE main setting type and ONE type of core professional.

Table 1
Unitary ECEC systems for children of all ages up to the beginning of primary schooling

	ONE lead ministry	ONE legal framework	ONE curricular framework	ONE main setting type	ONE type of core professional
Croatia	✓	✓	✓	✓	✓
Denmark	✓	✓	✓	✓	✓
Estonia	✓	✓	✓	✓	✓
Finland	✓	✓*	✓*	✓	In principle yes, but two types in legislation
Latvia	✓	✓	✓	✓	✓
Lithuania	✓	✓	✓*	✓	✓
Norway	✓	✓	✓	✓	✓
Slovenia	✓	✓	✓	✓	✓
Sweden	✓	✓	✓*	✓	✓
Ukraine	✓	✓	✓	✓	✓

*Separate for pre-primary class 6–7 years
Source: SEEPRO-3 country reports, in: Oberhuemer/Schreyer 2024b

Overall, ten of the 33 SEEPRO-3 countries fulfil the five criteria of a *unitary* ECEC system. Whereas the ECEC sectors in *Croatia, Denmark, Estonia, Latvia, Norway, Slovenia* and *Ukraine* fully meet all five criteria, it should be noted that the pre-primary classes for 6 to 7 year-olds in *Finland, Lithuania* and *Sweden* have a separate curricular framework and in *Finland* a separate legal framework for this latter part of the ECEC system. In *Finland*, too, two types of ECEC professional are mentioned in the relevant legislation: a 'Teacher in ECEC' and a 'Social Pedagogue in ECEC'. The former follows a three-year university study programme exclusively focused on ECEC. The latter has a university of applied sciences degree, of which only a relatively minor part is dedicated to ECEC, the remainder focusing on general social work. Both are classified as ISCED[4] 6 qualifications.

The situation becomes more complex in the *part-integrated* ECEC systems (see Table 2). Ten of the 33 countries can be described in this way.

Although all ECEC provision has been brought under the responsibility of one lead ministry in *Italy, Luxembourg, Malta, Romania, Serbia* and *Spain*, several of the other four criteria are not met in the same way. In *Serbia*, where the system is almost fully integrated, the only indicator not fulfilled is that of having one type of core professional across age groups. In *Italy*, the decision to merge the two previous sectors for children below and above the age of 3 into an 'integrated system' was made in 2015 and came into force in 2017. In the meantime, educational guidelines have been issued for the entire ECEC phase but the previous curricular frameworks are still valid and the ECEC setting types remain distinctly different. An important move was made to upgrade the minimum qualification requirement for staff working in services for under-threes to Bachelor level, but this is not the same formal requirement as that for teachers working in the *scuole dell'infanzia* for the 3, 4 and 5 year-olds, which is an ISCED 7 qualification, equivalent to a Master's degree. Another example is *Luxembourg* where, despite bringing both non-formal and formal ECEC together under the auspices of one lead ministry, the legal frameworks, curricula and core professionals in both remain distinctly different.

Also among the part-integrated ECEC systems are those in federally organised countries (*Austria, Germany, Russia*). In such cases, federal-level regulations co-exist with those at federal state level (*Länder*) or, in the case of *Russia*, with those at the level of the so-called 'subjects' of the Federation (provinces, republics, regions, autonomous republics, autonomous districts, cities of federal significance). In the *UK*, where responsibilities for ECEC are devolved from the central government in *England* to *Scotland, Wales* and *Northern Ireland,* each of the four nations has its own legal framework and curriculum and staffing regulations.

---

4 ISCED stands for International Standard Classification of Education – see Glossary for details.

Table 2
Part-integrated ECEC systems for children of all ages up to the beginning of primary schooling

	ONE lead ministry	ONE legal framework	ONE curricular framework	ONE main setting type	ONE type of core professional
Italy	✓	✓	Three	NO	NO
Luxembourg	✓	NO	NO	NO	NO
Malta	✓	NO*	(NO)	NO	NO
Romania	✓	✓	✓	NO	NO
Serbia	✓	✓	✓	✓	NO
Spain	✓	✓	✓	NO	NO
Federal and devolved ECEC systems					
Austria	One at federal level, 9 regional governments	Federation-*Länder* agreements with varying regulations	✓	NO	✓
Germany	One at federal level, 16 at *Länder* level	One at federal level, 16 at *Länder* level	One at cross-*Länder* level, 16 at *Länder* level	NO	✓
Russia	One at federal level, many at regional level	✓	✓	✓	NO
UK	Four separate top-level authorities	Four nation-specific legal frameworks	Four nation-specific curricula	NO	NO

*Although the existing types of legislation for each sector have not been merged in *Malta*, a National Policy Framework (2021) has been issued for the entire ECEC phase.
Source: SEEPRO-3 country reports, in: Oberhuemer/Schreyer 2024b

Although there has been a gradual move away from strictly *bi-sectoral* ('split') ECEC systems over the past ten years or so, they still account for more than a third (13) of the 33 SEEPRO-3 countries (see Table 3).

In *Belgium, Bulgaria, Cyprus, Czech Republic, France, Greece, Hungary, Ireland, The Netherlands, Poland, Portugal, Slovakia* and *Switzerland*, responsibilities for ECEC are divided. *France* is indicative of a split system of early childhood education and care, with two separate sectors, three responsible ministries and staff qualification requirements which differ both in formal terms and in professional orientation. *Belgium*, as a federal state with three language communities – Flemish, French and German-speaking – has a unique position within this group of countries. Not only does each language community have its own ECEC system, each with its own top-level authority and separate regulations, but within each of the three communities ECEC is provided in two different sectors. *Switzerland* is also a special case in that there is no one national top-level authority, and both childcare and education come exclusively under cantonal responsibility.

Table 3
Bi-sectoral ECEC systems for children of all ages up to the beginning of primary schooling

	ONE lead ministry	ONE legal framework	ONE curricular framework	ONE main setting type	ONE type of core professional
Bulgaria	NO	NO	NO	NO	NO
Cyprus	NO	NO	NO	NO	NO
Czech Rep.	NO	NO	NO	NO	NO
France	NO	NO	NO	NO	NO
Greece	NO	NO	NO	NO	NO
Hungary	NO	NO	NO	NO	NO
Ireland	NO	NO	NO	NO	NO
The Netherlands	NO	NO	NO	NO	NO
Poland	NO	NO	NO	NO	NO
Portugal	NO	NO	NO	NO	✓
Slovakia	NO	NO	NO	NO	NO
Federal and cantonal ECEC systems					
Belgium	3 top-level authorities	NO	NO	NO	NO
Switzerland	Cantonal responsibility	NO	NO	NO	NO

Source: SEEPRO-3 country reports, in: Oberhuemer/Schreyer 2024b

As to be expected within this system mix, there can be no singular definition of a core professional in terms of the tasks they are expected to fulfil and of their understanding of what it means to be an early childhood professional. A childcare worker in the predominantly privately-run settings in the *French Community of Belgium*, for example, with a minimum ISCED 3 qualification, is likely to have a very different professional self-image from a Master's educated teacher who is firmly embedded within the school education system, as in *Poland* or *Portugal*.

3 Key policy measures since the previous SEEPRO study

Since the publication of the last SEEPRO study in 2017/2018, a number of important steps have been taken in the 33 countries represented in the current study, particularly in relation to the governance of early childhood education and childcare systems, but also in terms of the ECEC workforce. This chapter provides a brief overview of significant changes since 2017, which are structured according to four key areas: legislative changes, curricular reforms, measures to facilitate access to early childhood education and personnel-related measures, followed by a short note about changes in the names of key ministries and jurisdictions.

3.1 Legislative changes

In the seven years since the last SEEPRO study, important legislative changes and amendments have taken place on key aspects of the ECEC systems.

In the ten countries with a *unitary* ECEC system, where most of the relevant laws relate specifically to the entire phase of early childhood education and care (and not just to parts of it, as in many other countries), legislative changes were made in seven countries.

- In *Denmark*, for example, additional specifications regarding the pedagogical framework, a stronger monitoring of the ECEC system and minimum standards for staffing ratios were included in the Early Childhood Education and Care Act in 2021. By 2024, at least one adult must be available for three children aged 0–2[5] years and six children aged 3–5 years.
- In *Estonia*, an amendment to the Early Childhood Education and Care Act focused on supporting children with special educational needs. In addition, a draft law was presented in 2022 to strengthen the integration of childcare services into the education system and thus complete the advanced integration of the education and care sectors. The law is expected to be passed by parliament in 2024.

---

5 **Note on age range format:** International data sources use varying ways of presenting the age range of children enrolled in ECEC settings. We have chosen the following format for the SEEPRO-3 reports and this book: **0–2** for children **up to** 3 years of age and **3–5** for 3, 4 and 5 year-olds in countries with a primary school entry age of 6 years. Depending on the specific setting features in each country, these may appear as **0–3** (under 4 year-olds), **0–5** (under 6 year-olds), **4–5** (4 and 5 year-olds), and so on.

- The right of every child to early childhood education has been reaffirmed in *Finland*; inclusive principles are now enshrined in legislation.
- In *Croatia*, amendments to the Early Childhood Education Act took place in 2019, 2022 and 2023. These aim, among other things, to ensure equal educational opportunities and inclusion for all, as well as respect for children's rights.
- In *Lithuania*, an amendment to the Education Act in 2020 forms the framework for the gradual entitlement to universal early education by 2025 for 4, 3 and 2 year-olds. The amendment also specifies the parents' right to choose their child's school entry age.
- In *Norway*, amendments to the Kindergarten Act in 2021 focus primarily on the prevention of discrimination.
- Amendments made in 2021 to the Early Education Act in *Ukraine* focus primarily on ensuring equal access to early childhood education.

In six of the ten countries with a *part-integrated* ECEC system, changes have also been made to the relevant laws since 2017.

- In *Germany*, the *Gute-KiTa-Gesetz* (Act on the Further Development of Quality and Participation in ECEC) came into force in 2019, the aims of which were to improve quality in ten fields of action and introduce new monitoring and evaluation measures in the 16 federal states with the help of substantial federal funding measures. Four years later, this strategy was continued through the ECEC Quality Act (*KiTa-Qualitätsgesetz*, 2023) with seven fields of action: needs-based provision; staff-child ratio; recruiting and binding qualified staff; strong leadership; language education; measures for child development, health, nutrition and exercise; strengthening home-based childcare. Each of the 16 federal states chooses its own priority fields and receives federal funding for this focus up to the end of 2024. The federal government is investing a total of four billion euros in these measures.
- In *Malta*, two pieces of legislation were added to the 1988 Education Act in 2019: The National Basic Curriculum, which defines the work in kindergartens for 3 and 4 year-olds, and the registration of childcare centres as educational institutions. National Standards for ECEC services (0–2 years) were published in 2021, which, among other things, are intended to ensure accessibility to high-quality services; also in 2021, the National Framework for ECEC in Malta and Gozo was issued, aimed at maximising children's development in the years before school enrolment at the age of 5.
- In *Luxembourg*, the subsidisation of childcare costs through vouchers was regulated by law in 2018 and mini-crèches were established as a new form of ECEC.

- Changes to the national education law in *Romania* emphasised the importance of education for children under 3 years of age. In 2020, the year before school enrolment (from the age of 5) became compulsory.
- In *Serbia*, the Early Education Act, which is based on the Fundamentals of the Education System Act, was updated in 2019 and 2020.
- The Education Act in *Spain*, which came into force in 2021, strengthens the first cycle of education for children under 3 years of age through specific pedagogical and evaluative guidelines for this first stage in the education system. Measures are also to be taken to increase the number of places for this age group and to promote gender equality in early education.

The following legislative amendments were reported for ten of the 13 countries with a *bi-sectoral* ECEC system:

- In *Belgium*, attending pre-primary education became compulsory from the age of 5 in 2020.
- In 2020, an amendment was made to the Early Education and Schools Act in *Bulgaria*: a three-year pre-primary education in kindergartens for 4 to under 7 year-olds was made compulsory from 2023.
- In *Cyprus*, the school entry age was raised to 5 years 10 months in 2020/21 and then to 6 years in 2021/22.
- The 2022 amendment to the *Czech Republic*'s Education Act primarily concerns language support for children aged 5 who are required to attend kindergarten.
- Since the law for a 'school of trust' came into force in July 2019, attendance at an *école maternelle* has been compulsory in *France* from the age of 3.
- From 2018 to 2021, the age for starting compulsory pre-primary education in *Greece* was gradually reduced to 4 years.
- The Education Act in *Ireland* was amended in 2021, emphasising parents' right to choose an ECEC facility as well as promoting equal opportunities, inclusion, lifelong learning and support for children's individual needs.
- In *The Netherlands*, two new laws were passed for the 0–3 age group. In 2018, both the 'Innovation and Quality of Childcare Act' and the 'Harmonisation of Work in Childcare and Playgroups Act' came into force, primarily intended to improve the quality and accessibility of childcare. In addition, in terms of multilingual childcare, legislation stipulates that from 2024, ECEC services can offer a maximum of 50% of daily childcare hours in German, French or English.
- In *Portugal*, Law 54/2018 reorganised the inclusion of children with special educational needs, with the main aim of providing all children with the support they need and placing them in mainstream facilities whenever possible. Since 2018, there has also been a legal entitlement for over 3 year-olds to a free place for 25 hours per week. From 2022, a new legal framework provides for the gradual expansion of free access to ECEC by 2024.

- In 2021, the Education Act in *Slovakia* was amended to abolish the so-called 'zero classes' for 5 year-olds from socially disadvantaged and low-income backgrounds and to introduce compulsory kindergarten from the age of 5. In addition, a legal entitlement to a place in kindergarten is to be introduced for all 4 year-olds from 2024 and for all 3 year-olds from 2025.

3.2 Curricular reforms

In four of the ten countries with a *unitary* ECEC system, a number of amendments to the curricular framework have been introduced since 2017.

- In *Denmark*, for example, the previous framework curriculum was revised in 2018 by a group of experts, stakeholders and ECEC staff and adopted as 'The enhanced pedagogical curriculum'. This involved expanding the content focus and also explicitly defining leadership responsibilities. These now include, for example, supervising the creation of a centre-specific education plan to be approved by the respective local authority, as well as an annual evaluation of this with the involvement of the advisory board.
- In *Latvia*, a group of experts has also developed new curricular guidelines, which now serve as an orientation template for centre-specific education plans.
- In *Sweden*, the fourth revision of the preschool curriculum came into force in 2018. On the one hand, play is emphasised as the basis for development, learning and wellbeing; at the same time, the term 'teaching' was introduced for the first time, presumably to make it clear that *förskolan* are part of the education system. In addition, a greater focus was placed on literacy, maths, science and technology, as well as on cooperation with parents (Williams et al. 2018).
- Following a revision by experts with a research or practical background, the 'Basic Component of Early Education' has become the early education framework curriculum in *Ukraine* since 2021. The document describes the skills that children should have at the end of early childhood education and gives inclusive education high priority.

Among the countries with a *part-integrated* ECEC system, five countries and three of the British nations report amendments to the curricular framework.

- In *England (UK)*, the Statutory Framework for the Early Years Foundation Stage was revised in 2021, emphasising play and exploration, active learning and creative and critical thinking.
- In *Germany*, the Common Framework for Early Education in ECEC Centres adopted by the Conference of Ministers of Education and Youth of the

16 federal states in 2004 was updated in 2022. The basic principles of this non-binding framework include a holistic approach to learning, the participation of children in decision-making processes, intercultural pedagogy and gender-sensitive pedagogical work.
- Pedagogical guidelines for the newly integrated 0–6 system in *Italy* were adopted by the Ministry of Education in 2021. They define both the cultural and pedagogical framework of early education programmes and recommend a unified and holistic approach to the education of children from the first year of life up to the age of 6. In addition, national guidelines were published in 2022 specifically for educational practice in ECEC services for children under the age of 3.
- In *Romania*, too, a new early education curriculum, issued in 2019, has taken into account the entire early childhood phase for 0 to under 6 year-olds for the first time. In particular, it emphasises child-centred education, respect for children's rights, active learning, integrated development, interculturality, equality and equal rights as well as education as a relationship-building interaction between professionals and children.
- In 2018, a new conceptual framework for early childhood education ('Years of Ascent') was developed in *Serbia* in a collaborative venture. It is based on contemporary theories on childhood and curricula, early learning and early childhood development, as well as on cross-national analyses of curricular documents and examples of 'best practice' in high-quality early education programmes worldwide.
- In 2022, a royal decree in *Spain* explicated the regulations and content of the first education cycle (0–2) in more detail: promoting children's development, personal autonomy, a positive self-image and education in civic values.
- While the previous statutory curriculum framework in *Wales (UK)* for working with 3 to 7 year olds (Foundation Phase Framework) applied to both private and state ECEC centres, a new 'Curriculum for Wales' has been in place since 2022, which applies to all schools (and thus only state maintained nursery provision), giving them the opportunity to design their own education plan around four core aims: ambitious and competent learners; imaginative and creative contributors; ethical and informed citizens; healthy and confident individuals.
- The Curriculum, Examinations and Assessment Council in *Northern Ireland (UK)* published revised curriculum guidelines for early education in 2018. These emphasise the opportunity to develop individual potential within a holistic approach.

In the 13 countries with a *bi-sectoral* ECEC system, comparatively fewer curricular changes were reported – only in four cases.

- In the *Czech Republic*, a revision of the framework education programme for kindergartens (3–5 years) was started in 2023 with the aim of working more according to a child-centred pedagogy, including active learning, discovering the world and building independence and autonomy in the context of democratic and humanistic values.
- In *France*, the national charter for childcare (2021) provides the first curricular guidance for crèches and other childcare services (0–2 years). For *écoles maternelles* (2–5 years), the Ministry of Education and Youth launched a new plan in 2023 aiming for the 'success' and 'flourishing' of children through continuity in early education, strengthening relationships with parents and improving the transition to primary school.
- A revision of the national curriculum for kindergartens took place in *Greece* in 2022, which included the introduction of English and digital technologies in pre-primary education.
- In *Ireland*, consultations with decision-makers in the non-school sector have been taking place since 2022 to revise the 'Aistear' early years curriculum. For the education sector, a new framework curriculum for primary and special schools was published in March 2023, which builds on earlier curricula but also addresses changing needs and priorities.

3.3 Measures to improve access to ECEC

- In *Bulgaria*, parental contributions for kindergarten attendance for 4 to under 7 year-olds were abolished entirely in 2021.
- From April 2024, 15 hours of childcare per week were made free for all children aged 9 months and over for working parents in *England (UK)*. From September 2025, this entitlement is to be extended to 30 hours for children under 5 years of age.
- In *Ireland*, the introduction of a new national childcare programme in 2019 reduced childcare costs for parents.
- In *The Netherlands*, the length of attendance at an ECEC centre for disadvantaged children aged between 2½ and 4 was increased from 10 hours a week to 16 hours in 2019.
- In *Norway*, low-income families have been entitled to 20 hours of free kindergarten attendance for children under the age of 2 since 2019.
- In *Scotland (UK)*, all 3 and 4 year-olds and all eligible 2 year-olds have received 1,140 hours of free early learning and care per year since 2021.
- In *Slovenia*, parents with two children no longer have to pay a kindergarten fee for the younger child.

3.4 Personnel-related measures

Many of the more recent staff-related measures are described in more detail in other chapters of this book and especially in the SEEPRO-3 ECEC Workforce Profile reports (https://www.seepro.eu). Only a brief overview of selected changes is given here.

- In 2019, three-year vocational schools were introduced in *Austria* for the training of Pedagogical Assistants. Since 2020, career changers can enrol on courses in early childhood education at universities for teacher education which, since 2022, have also introduced courses of four semesters in 'inclusive early childhood education'.
- In *Croatia*, the professional standard for ECEC core professionals was entered in the register of the Croatian Qualifications Framework in 2023.
- In the *Czech Republic*, an amendment to the Pedagogical Staff Act of 2023 defines the requirements for the qualification of pedagogical staff, working hours, further training and the career framework.
- In 2019/2020, a Bachelor's degree in Educational Science became mandatory in *Italy* for professionals working with under 3 year-olds.
- Kindergarten Educators (I and II) in *Malta* have been required to have at least an ISCED/EQF level 5 qualification (instead of ISCED 4) since 2021. Also in 2021, National Standards for Child Daycare Facilities were published, which set the minimum qualification level for staff in ECEC services for children up to 3 years of age.
- In *Serbia*, a set of regulations on competence standards for ECEC Teachers was adopted in 2018.
- In *Slovakia*, the Act on Teaching and Professional Support Staff updated the professional development programme for these staff working with children aged 3 and over in 2019, including specifications on mandatory and optional forms and modalities of certification. From 2023, kindergarten professionals have been required to attend a mandatory course in pre-primary education of 50 to 100 hours, which must be completed within seven years of starting employment as a pedagogical professional.
- In *Slovenia*, ECEC Teachers have had the opportunity to become Senior Councillors since 2022 through the creation of a fourth promotion title and Early Childhood Education Assistants can apply for the positions of Mentor or Adviser for the first time. The Ministry of Education and the relevant trade union agreed to significantly increase the salaries of Early Childhood Education Assistants in 2023.

Supplementary note: Changes at the national ministry level

In five countries, formal changes took place at the level of the responsible national authority.
- In *Denmark*, this involved a change of ministry: in 2020, following a new government, ECEC centres came under the auspices of the Ministry of Children and Education, whereas they previously had had a long history of being the responsibility of the Ministry of Social Affairs.
- According to the draft law on early childhood education and care in *Estonia* in 2022, not only ECEC centres/kindergartens for children aged 1½ to 7 years, but also childcare services are to come under the overall responsibility of the Ministry of Education and Research.
- In *Spain*, a new Ministry for Youth and Childhood was established in 2023. However, the early childhood education centres of the first (0–2 years) and second (3–5 years) cycles are still the responsibility of the Ministry of Education.
- In 2018, the Ministry of Education and Science in *Romania* was split into two: Ministry of Education and Ministry of Science and Higher Education.
- Conversely, in *Poland*, the Ministry of National Education was again merged with the Ministry of Science and Higher Education in 2021 and renamed the Ministry of Education and Science.

4 Contextual Framework

4.1 Legal entitlement and compulsory enrolment in ECEC

In almost all 33 countries in the SEEPRO-3 study, children have a *right* to a place in an ECEC setting, at least from a certain, legally defined age. In some cases, this entitlement arises from the increasing number of countries that have opted for *compulsory* attendance, usually for the year before school enrolment – sometimes for two or three years before primary schooling. This chapter provides an overview of these two different strategies for providing and guaranteeing places.

4.1.1 Legal entitlement to a place in an ECEC setting

In the vast majority of SEEPRO-3 countries, children have a universal legal entitlement to attend an ECEC centre from a specific age. The starting age varies from country to country and is defined by law. In such cases, the responsible authorities and municipalities are obliged to guarantee a place for the children in this specified age group whose parents wish to enrol them.

Italy is the only country without a legal entitlement or eligibility specification to attend ECEC. In *Ireland* there is currently no legal entitlement, but children from 2 years 8 months are eligible to attend settings providing an 'Early Childhood Care and Education (ECCE)' programme free of charge for three hours per day for 38 weeks/year over a period of two years. In *Malta*, eligibility for under 3 year-olds is also not universal, but restricted to working or studying parents; in the *UK* nations it is restricted to certain age and target groups.

While in the majority of countries this legal entitlement or eligibility does not begin until the children are 3 or 4 years old, in 11 countries (*Denmark, Germany, Estonia, Finland, Latvia, Malta, Norway, Russia, Sweden, Slovenia, Ukraine*) it applies to children from a very early age: in *Russia* and *Ukraine* from 2 months, in *Denmark* from 26 weeks, in *Slovenia* from 11 months and in *Germany, Norway* and *Sweden* from 1 year.

In a few countries, a legal entitlement was introduced over 20, 30 or even more years ago: in the *Flemish* and *French Communities of Belgium* by the end of the 1960s, in *Slovenia* in 1987, in *Denmark* and *Finland* in 1996 and in *Sweden* in 1999. Some of the framework conditions for this have changed over the years. In *Denmark*, for example, the legal entitlement for working parents first introduced in 1996 was extended to a universal place guarantee for all parents in 2004 (Larsen/de la Porte 2022). In *Finland*, the universal legal entitlement introduced in 1996 for all children before school enrolment was somewhat restricted between 2016 and 2020, but since 2020 the subjective right of every child to early childhood education and care has been restored (Chydenius 2024).

To provide an overview, we have structured the countries according to the three types of ECEC system (unitary, part-integrated, bi-sectoral). Some differences are noticeable: In the countries with a *unitary* ECEC system (see Table 4), the legal entitlement tends to start earlier than in the countries with a part-integrated or bi-sectoral system (see Tables 5 and 6). These unified systems also include the most examples of later school entry at the age of 7 (*Estonia, Finland, Croatia, Latvia, Sweden*). This gives children the guaranteed opportunity to attend the same ECEC setting for a longer period of time than in the other systems - with the advantages of continuity and fewer unnecessary breaks in the early educational biography.

In total, there are nine SEEPRO-3 countries with a school entry age of 7 years (*Bulgaria, Croatia, Estonia, Finland, Latvia, Poland, Russia, Serbia* and *Sweden*). Only in *Malta* and the nations of the *United Kingdom* is primary school compulsory for 5 year-olds (with children often starting at the age of 4) and in Northern Ireland for 4 year-olds. In all other countries (22 in total), compulsory primary education begins at the age of 6.

Table 4
Legal entitlement (LE) in unitary ECEC systems (2023/24)

Country	Start of primary schooling in years	Start of LE or eligibility in months/years	Starting year of LE or eligibility	Notes
Croatia	7[1]	5 or 6	2014	250 hours/year before primary school *compulsory*
Denmark	6	26 weeks	1996 2004	Chargeable full-time place in a publicly subsidised ECEC setting (*no compulsory enrolment*)
Estonia	7	1½	2014	ECEC places free of charge (*no compulsory enrolment*)
Finland	7	approx. 9 months	1996	Between 2016 and 2020, LE was limited to 20 hours/week and was only for unemployed parents or parents on parenting leave; since 2020, universal LE has been restored. One year before primary school *compulsory*
Latvia	7	1½	2011	Two years before primary school *compulsory*

Country	Start of primary schooling in years	Start of LE or eligibility in months/years	Starting year of LE or eligibility	Notes
Lithuania	6	3	2023	Up to 2023/24, primary schooling began at age 7. Successive changes since 2020. As from 2025, LE to be extended to 2 year-olds (one year before primary school *compulsory*)
		2	2024	
Norway	6	1	2009	Up to 41 hours/week (*no compulsory enrolment*)
Sweden	7	1	1999	Guaranteed hours: 525 per year from the age of 3 (one year before primary school *compulsory*)
Slovenia	6	11 months	1987	(*No compulsory enrolment*)
Ukraine	6	2 months	2021	(*No compulsory enrolment*)

[1] Children born between January and March start school in the calendar year in which they turn 6; all others in the year in which they turn 7.
Sources: SEEPRO-3 Key Contextual Data synopses, in: Oberhuemer/Schreyer 2024b; Larsen/de la Porte 2022; European Commission/EACEA/Eurydice 2023

Table 5
Legal entitlement (LE) in part-integrated ECEC systems (2023/24)

Country	Start of primary schooling in years	Start of LE or eligibility in months/years	Starting year of LE or eligibility	Notes
Austria	6	5	2009	No LE before the one year of 20 hours per week *compulsory enrolment*
Germany	6	1	2013	Guaranteed hours and parental fees vary across the federal states (*no compulsory enrolment*)
Italy	6		No legal entitlement	
Luxembourg	6	3/4	2009	Guaranteed hours for 36 hours/week for children between 3 and 4 years of age in the formal education sector; *compulsory enrolment* for 4 and 5 year-olds for 28 hours per week during the school year (*no compulsory enrolment* in non-formal sector)

Country	Start of primary schooling in years	Start of LE or eligibility in months/years	Starting year of LE or eligibility	Notes
Malta	5 (4 years, 9 months)	3 months	2014	Only parents of under 3 year-olds who are in employment or studying are eligible for a place in a childcare centre. Kindergarten from 2 years 9 months free of charge (*no compulsory enrolment*)
Romania	6	4	2023	2 years *compulsory enrolment*, from 2030: 3 years
Russia	7	2 months	2012	LE from 2 months; ECEC free of charge from 3 years onwards (*no compulsory enrolment*)
Serbia	7	6	2006	No LE before a one-year (at least 9 months) *compulsory enrolment* before primary education
Spain	6	3	2006	Guaranteed hours: 25 per week, in some Autonomous Communities from the age of 1 or 2 (*no compulsory enrolment*)
United Kingdom (UK), England	5	2* 3**	1998 4 year-olds 2004 3 year-olds 2013 2 year-olds	Guaranteed hours 2023: 15 per week free of charge for 38 weeks a year for all 3 and 4 year-olds and for some 2 year-olds; 30 hours per week for 3 and 4 year-olds with parents in employment. From September 2024: 15 hours/week and from September 2025 30 hours/week from the age of 9 months for children with working parents (*no compulsory enrolment*)
UK Wales	5	2/3 ***	ca. 2004	12½ hours per week free of charge for 39 weeks/year for 2 and 3 year-olds from disadvantaged areas; 30 hours/week; 30 hours per week for 48 weeks/year for 3 and 4 year-olds with working parents (*no compulsory enrolment*)
UK Scotland	5	2*/3	2002 3 and 4 year-olds	Since August 2021: 30 hours/week during the school year (1,140 hours/year) free of charge for all 3 and 4 year-olds and eligible 2 year-olds (*no compulsory enrolment*)

Country	Start of primary schooling in years	Start of LE or eligibility in months/years	Starting year of LE or eligibility	Notes
UK N. Ireland	4	3**	ca. 2004	12½ hours/week during the school year for 3 year-olds (*no compulsory enrolment*)

*Targeted **only during the school year** either targeted or only during the school year
Sources: SEEPRO-3 Key Contextual Data synopses, in: Oberhuemer/Schreyer 2024b

Table 6
Legal entitlement (LE) in bi-sectoral ECEC systems (2023/24)

Country	Start of primary schooling in years	Start of LE or eligibility in months/years	Starting year of LE or eligibility	Notes
Belgium	6	2½	1969* *BE-nl, BE-fr* 2024 *BE-de* (previously 3 years)	One year *compulsory enrolment*
Bulgaria	7	4	2023	Successive extension of *compulsory enrolment* since 2020
Cyprus	6	5	2018	No LE before one year *compulsory enrolment* for 26 hours/week
Czech Republic	6	3	2016 2017 2018	Successive introduction first for 5 year-olds, then 4 and 3 year-olds (one year *compulsory enrolment*)[1]
France	6	3	2019	Three years *compulsory enrolment*
Greece	6	4	2021	2 years *compulsory* enrolment for 25 hours/week
Hungary	6	3	2016	4 hours a day *compulsory enrolment*
Ireland	6	2 years 8 months	2016	Guaranteed hours: 3 per day for 76 weeks in settings providing the cost-free *Early Childhood Care and Education* programme (*no compulsory enrolment*)

35

Country	Start of primary schooling in years	Start of LE or eligibility in months/years	Starting year of LE or eligibility	Notes
The Netherlands	6	4	1985	LE for 4 year-olds, one year of *compulsory enrolment* for 5 year-olds in a *basisschool*, usually for 20 hours per week free of charge. *Local authority duty*: to provide 16 hours in a childcare centre for 2½ to 4 year-olds; fees charged and very expensive
Poland	7	3	2017	Guaranteed hours: at least 25 per week (one year *compulsory enrolment*)
Portugal	6	3	2018	Guaranteed hours: 25 per week (*no compulsory enrolment*)
Slovakia	6	4 3	2024/25 2025/26	Successive introduction of LE (one year *compulsory enrolment*)
Switzerland	6/7	4	Varies across cantons	LE for under 4 year-olds only in the city of Basel; otherwise *compulsory enrolment* the norm for 4 and 5 year-olds, with variations across cantons in terms of length and number of hours (and in some German-speaking cantons *no compulsory enrolment*)

[1]Two years are compulsory for children whose entry into primary education has been deferred.
* Although there was never a legal obligation ('entitlement') for children to attend, from the late 1960s onwards nearly all Belgian children were enrolled in an ECEC centre, in most cases on a full-time basis (Willekens/Scheiwe 2020: 15).
Sources: General Secretariat EDK 2007; SEEPRO-3 Key Contextual Data synopses, in: Oberhuemer/Schreyer 2024b

Compared to the data in the SEEPRO-r report published in 2017/18 (Oberhuemer/Schreyer 2018), the framework conditions for legal entitlement have remained unchanged in eight countries (*Denmark, Estonia, Germany, Hungary, Italy, Latvia, Luxembourg, Spain*) as well as in the *Flemish Community of Belgium* and in *Northern Ireland (United Kingdom)*. In other countries, however, the age from which legal entitlement is granted was lowered during this period (e.g. in *Bulgaria, Lithuania, Malta, Slovakia*) or modalities such as the duration of attendance were changed. In *Poland* and *Portugal*, for example, the number of hours was set at 25 per week.

4.1.2 Compulsory enrolment in an ECEC setting

In countries which have introduced compulsory enrolment in ECEC, local authorities are obliged to offer places for all children in the legally defined age group.

The compulsory strategy is a relatively new phenomenon for the majority of the countries that have chosen this path and was only introduced after 2015 in most cases. In two countries, however, there is also a long tradition of compulsory enrolment: in *Luxembourg*, attending a pre-primary class has been compulsory for 5 year-olds since 1976 and for 4 year-olds since 1992; and attending a kindergarten class in the *basisschool* in *The Netherlands* became compulsory for 5 year-olds in 1985. However, the reasons and objectives for compulsory enrolment are similar in all countries: the aim is to provide better support for children from families living in disadvantaged conditions, to offer targeted language education and generally to work towards a successful transition to primary school.

Overall, attending an ECEC centre is compulsory for a legally defined length of time in 21 of the 33 SEEPRO-3 countries. Table 7 orders them according to the duration in years. Only in three countries (*Bulgaria, France and Hungary*) does compulsory attendance at an early childhood education centre last three years (although in *France*, strictly speaking, it is 'instruction' that is compulsory, not necessarily attendance at an *école maternelle*) (Rayna 2024). In five countries (*Greece, Latvia, Luxembourg, Romania, Switzerland*), two years of compulsory enrolment before starting primary education are the norm. In most (11) of these countries (*Austria, Belgium, Croatia, Cyprus, Finland, Lithuania, The Netherlands, Poland, Serbia, Slovakia, Sweden*), one year of compulsory enrolment is required. In the *Czech Republic* and *Ukraine*, attendance is compulsory for one or two years – two years in the former for children who have been deferred from school, in the latter for children with special needs.

In most countries (13), a certain mandatory number of hours per week is set for educational activities: usually around 20 to 25 hours per week. In *Lithuania*, for example, 20 hours a week or 640 hours a year are compulsory; in *Serbia*, four hours a day for at least nine months before school enrolment; in *Finland*, 700 hours in pre-school classes for 6 to 7 year-olds.

Table 7
Compulsory enrolment in 21 SEEPRO-3 countries (2023/24)

Country (primary school starting age)	Starting age compulsory enrolment	Length of compulsory enrolment in years	Introduced in...	Number of compulsory hours
Bulgaria (7)	4	3	2023	4 to 5 year-olds: 13 pedagogical units per week; 5 to 6 year-olds: 15 units; 6 to 7 year-olds: 17 units
France (6)	3	3	2019	27 hours/week: 6 hours daily except on Wednesdays (3 hours)
Hungary (6)	3	3	2011	4 hours/day
Greece (6)	4	2	2021	25 hours/week
Latvia (7)	5	2	1999	Not specified
Luxembourg (6)	4	2	1976: 5 y. 1992: 4 y.	28 hours/week for 4 and 5 year-olds during school year
Romania (6)	4	2	2023	
Switzerland (6/7)	4	1 in 8 cantons; 2 in 18 cantons	2008 in Zurich, varies across cantons	Number of hours and exact age vary across cantons
Czech Republic (6)	5	1 or 2[1]	2017	20 hours/week
Ukraine (6)	5	1 or 2[2]	2017	
Belgium (6)	5	1	2020; 2024	BE-fr: 23 hours/week; BE-nl: 23-33 hours/week; BE-de: 28 x 50 mins./week
Finland (7)	6	1	2015	At least 700 hours of educational activities
Croatia (7)[3]	6	1	2014	250 hours/year
Lithuania (6)	6	1	2016	20 hours/week
The Netherlands (6)	5	1	1985	Usually 20 hours/week
Austria (6)	5	1	2018	At least 20 hours/week
Poland (7)	6	1	2017	At least 25 hours/week
Sweden (7)	6	1	2018	525 hours/year
Slovakia (6)	5	1	2021	At least 4 hours/day
Cyprus (6)	5	1	2018	26 hours/week
Serbia (7)	5½/6	1	2006	4 hours/day over the school year (i.e. 9 months)

[1] For children with deferred school entry [2] For children with special educational needs
[3] Children born between January and March start school in the calendar year in which they turn 6; all others in the year in which they turn 7.
Sources: General Secretariat EDK 2007; SEEPRO-3 Key Contextual Data synopses, in: Oberhuemer/Schreyer 2024b

4.1.3 Countries with no compulsory enrolment

In 12 of the 33 SEEPRO-3 countries – *Denmark, Estonia, Germany, Ireland, Italy, Malta, Norway, Portugal, Russia, Slovenia, Spain, United Kingdom* – there are no legal provisions for compulsory enrolment in ECEC.

4.2 ECEC providers and main setting types

4.2.1 Provider distribution across ECEC settings

Early childhood education and care facilities are operated and organised by various providers. On the one hand, these can be public bodies, such as local authorities or municipalities or, in some countries, the state. On the other hand, private providers can also be responsible for ECEC centres – for example, private non-profit organisations, including church-affiliated providers, but also private-commercial agencies. Depending on the country, ECEC system and age group of the children enrolled, the distribution of providers varies.

In the SEEPRO-3 project, data were collected on the distribution of the respective ECEC centres by provider and also on the distribution of children across settings run by different providers. As a rule, however, these two data sources are closely linked, so that these differences are not discussed below.

In nine of the ten countries with a *unitary* ECEC system, the majority of providers of settings for children up to school age are public (between 70.2% in *Sweden* and 96.4% in *Ukraine*). In *Norway*, on the other hand, only just under half (48.3%) are public.

In eight of the ten countries with a *part-integrated* system, ECEC services for the over-3 age group are publicly managed. In *Germany*, on the other hand, almost two thirds of ECEC centres for 0 to 6 year-olds are privately owned (predominantly private non-profit); and in the *United Kingdom*, most providers of non-school ECEC centres for over 3 year-olds are private (in *England* mainly private-commercial).

With the exception of the *Flemish* and *German-speaking communities in Belgium, Cyprus, Ireland* and *The Netherlands*, the majority of settings attended by over 3 year-olds in the *bi-sectoral* ECEC systems are run by public providers.

Data on the provider affiliation of settings for under 3 year-olds is not available in all countries, or these shares are linguistically described as 'mainly' or 'mostly', or they are subsumed in an overall value for the age group from 0 years to school entry.

The latter is the case in countries with *unitary* ECEC systems such as *Denmark, Sweden* and *Ukraine*. For the remaining countries, the shares of public providers range from 48.3% (*Norway*) to 93.6% (*Slovenia*).

In some countries with a *part-integrated* system (*Germany, Serbia, England* and *Wales*) there is also an overall value for both age groups; no data for under 3 year-olds are available for *Russia*. In the remaining countries, ECEC settings attended by under-3s are more often run by private providers – from just over half in *Austria* (50.1%) and *Spain* (50.4%) to 91.5% in *Malta*.

In the countries with a *bi-sectoral* ECEC system, settings for under 3 year-olds are predominantly privately run, ranging from 53.2% in *Greece* to 77% in *Portugal*. One exception is *Hungary*, where the majority of family crèches are run by private non-profit organisations (89.1%), while traditional crèches and mini-crèches are almost exclusively run by the public sector (91.9% and 86.9%, respectively).

Overall, it can be noted that the proportion of public providers for facilities for under 3 year-olds is not as high as it is for the group of older children and in some cases is only slightly above 50% (e.g. in *Austria, Norway, Greece, Spain*). Furthermore, in the *part-integrated* and *bi-sectoral* systems, private providers appear to be the rule for ECEC provision for this age group.

4.2.2 ECEC setting types

Looking across all 33 SEEPRO countries, it is not only the provider types of ECEC settings that differ, but also the age of the children who attend them. For example, there are facilities solely (or predominantly) for under 3 year-olds, traditionally referred to as nurseries or crèches, settings solely for the 3–5 age group until they start school, or multi-age settings that accept children of all ages up to the start of primary education.

In the ten SEEPRO-3 countries with a *unitary* ECEC system, the majority of settings are multi-age centres, attended by children from the age of one until they start school. Within these facilities, however, the children are sometimes divided into specific age groups, such as in *Croatia*, where the kindergartens are either free-standing or attached to schools and are organised into three age bands (6 months to 1 year; 1 to 3 years and from 3 years until school entry). In *Sweden*, the under 3 year-olds and over 3 year-olds are usually in separate groups, but there are also facilities with mixed-age groups. In some countries, there are also pre-primary classes/groups for children in the year before compulsory schooling (e.g. in *Finland, Lithuania, Sweden*), which are often attached to schools and are usually compulsory (see also chapter 4.1.2). Additional alternative services round off the types of provision: for example, Sami facilities in *Finland*, Montessori settings in *Croatia* or school kindergartens in *Lithuania*.

In the ten countries with a *part-integrated* ECEC system, there are generally separate facilities for children under and above 3 or 4 years of age. Where capacity allows, 2 year-olds are often also admitted to the latter. In most of these countries, however, there are also multi-age facilities, e.g. in *Austria, Germany, Luxembourg* (non-formal sector)*, Russia, Serbia, Spain* and *UK-England* (Children's Centres). Only in *Italy* and *Malta* are there no regular ECEC centres that are explicitly designed as multi-age settings, although in *Italy* they are planned (see chapter 10.3).

In the 13 countries with a *bi-sectoral* ECEC system, age-segregated centres predominate due to the system type. In *France*, crèches are also categorised according to size: *micro-crèches* (with up to 12 places), *petites crèches* (13–24), *crèches* (25–39), *grandes crèches* (40–59) and *très grandes crèches* (over 60 places). In *Hungary*, mini-crèches are set up when there are not enough children in this age group to form a regular crèche. Family crèches care for children as young as 20 weeks and workplace crèches are mainly attended by children of employees of a particular company. In addition, in some countries (e.g. *Cyprus*, the *Czech Republic*, *Hungary, Ireland),* the childcare sector also offers multi-age programmes up to school entry, some of which are offered in parallel to pre-primary classes in schools (e.g. in *Ireland*). Alternative forms also exist, such as multifunctional centres or short-term childcare services in *France* with very flexible care for under 3 year-olds tailored to parental needs or, in the *Czech Republic* and *Slovakia*, forest or nature kindergartens or kindergartens that work according to the Montessori approach.

The proportion of children attending ECEC centres varies greatly across countries. For children under the age of 3, the range in enrolment rates (2022) is extreme: While only 2.3% attend an ECEC setting in *Slovakia*, almost three quarters (74.4%) of this age group are enrolled in *Denmark*. In contrast, the range in attendance rates for over 3 year-olds is much smaller: the lowest rate for this age group is found in *Serbia* at 61.6%, while in *Hungary* all children over the age of 3 attend a kindergarten.

According to the 'Barcelona targets' established by the European Commission in 2002, it was recommended that 33% of children under the age of 3 and 90% of children between the age of 3 and primary school entry participate in early childhood education and care. The enrolment rates in 2022 suggest that these targets were achieved for under 3 year-olds in 15 SEEPRO-3 countries and for over 3 or 4 year-olds in almost two thirds (21 countries). However, these recommended targets were increased in the revised 'Barcelona targets for 2030' (European Commission 2022) to 50% and 96%, respectively. Looking at the 2022 enrolment rates, these would only have been achieved by nine and five SEEPRO-3 countries, respectively.

4.3 Curricular frameworks – digital education

A series of international thematic reports of the *OECD Education 2030* project focuses on curriculum (re)design across education systems. Although not specifically about ECEC curricula, the insights gained from looking at curricula in various countries also have relevance for the early childhood field. It is emphasised that there is no universal consensus in terms of a defining concept of curriculum and that it is in fact often a contested concept. The *Education 2030* project concludes that curricula should aim to be inclusive, multi-layered, dynamic, holistic and multi-directional (OECD 2020: 11).

As a rule, curricula contain educational objectives and content, pedagogical guidelines and, in some cases, assessment guidelines. In many countries, there is a main document that is supplemented by additional documents with specific orientations, such as supporting children with special educational needs. Whether or not it is compulsory to apply the curriculum varies across countries (OECD 2020; European Commission/EACEA/Eurydice 2023). Most countries in the SEEPRO-3 study develop their own centre-specific pedagogical programme based on available national or regional frameworks.

4.3.1 Curricular frameworks according to ECEC system types

Tables 8, 9 and 10 present an overview of curricular frameworks according to ECEC system type, looking in particular at whether a curriculum is in place and whether or not it is legally binding for ECEC providers and settings.

In the ten countries with a *unitary* ECEC system (Table 8), the curricula apply to the entire age group up to primary school entry. Just over half of these countries have either separate curricula (Finland, Lithuania, Sweden) or age-focused specifications (Croatia, Estonia, Latvia) for the year or two preceding primary schooling.

Table 8
Curricular frameworks in unitary ECEC systems

Country and age group	Compulsory across the entire ECEC phase	Separate or age-focused specifications for pre-primary class or compulsory pre-primary groups
Croatia 0–5	✓	✓
Denmark 0–5	✓	Not applicable
Estonia 0–6	✓	✓
Finnland 0–6	✓	✓
Latvia 0–6	✓	✓
Lithuania 0–6	✓	✓

Country and age group	Compulsory across the entire ECEC phase	Separate or age-focused specifications for pre-primary class or compulsory pre-primary groups
Norway 0–5	✓	Not applicable
Slovenia 0–5	✓	Not applicable
Sweden 0–5	✓	✓
Ukraine 0–5	✓	Not applicable

Source: SEEPRO-3 country reports, in: Oberhuemer/Schreyer 2024b

In nearly all countries with a *part-integrated* system (Table 9), a curriculum for work with under 3 year-olds has been issued which, depending on the current state of integration, is either separate (*Luxembourg, Malta, Spain, UK-Scotland*) or is covered in an overall curriculum for the early childhood phase (*Austria, Germany, Italy, Romania, Russia, Serbia* as well as *UK-England* and *UK-Northern Ireland*). In *Germany*, there are 16 different curricula corresponding to the 16 federal states, which all cover the early childhood phase, but also in some case go beyond this to include work with children in out-of-school settings up to the age of 12. They are compulsory only in four federal states (Bavaria, Brandenburg, Saxony-Anhalt, Thuringia). An additional 'common framework', issued in 2004 by all 16 ministers of education and family affairs and updated in 2022, is not mandatory. In countries with compulsory pre-school groups or classes, age-focused specifications are usually issued for the final one or two years in an ECEC setting, as, for example, in Austria.

It is interesting to note that in a few countries with *part-integrated* systems, the curriculum has been chosen as a tool for creating a more integrated system and coordinating previously separate sectors, as in *Romania*.

Table 9
Curricular frameworks in part-integrated ECEC systems

Country	Compulsory for under 3 or under 4 year-olds	Compulsory for 3/4 year-olds and above
Austria		✓*
Germany	In four of the 16 *Länder* (Bavaria, Brandenburg, Saxony-Anhalt, Thuringia)	
Italy	✓	✓
	Guidelines for the new 0–6 integrated system	
Luxembourg	✓*	✓
Malta	✓	✓
Romania		✓
Russia		✓
Serbia		✓
Spain	✓	✓
UK – England		✓

Country	Compulsory for under 3 or under 4 year-olds	Compulsory for 3/4 year-olds and above
UK – Wales	NO	✓
UK - Scotland	NO	✓
UK – Northern Ireland		✓

Austria: Additional specifications for language learning and the compulsory pre-primary year; *Luxembourg:* for under 4 year-olds
Source: SEEPRO-3 country reports, in: Oberhuemer/Schreyer 2024b

As Table 10 illustrates, no curricular frameworks for the younger age group (up to 3 or 4 years of age) have been issued in five (*Cyprus, Czech Republic, Poland, Portugal, Slovakia*) of the 13 countries with a *bi-sectoral* ECEC system. Only three have a legally binding framework (*Belgium-fr, France and Hungary*). Otherwise, available guidelines are non-compulsory and issued as an orientation (*Belgium-nl, Belgium-de, Bulgaria, Greece, Ireland, The Netherlands, Switzerland*).

Table 10
Curricular frameworks in bi-sectoral ECEC systems

	Under 3 year-olds ✓ compulsory • non-compulsory X no guidelines/curricula	3 years and above* ✓ compulsory
Belgium-nl	•	✓*
Belgium-fr	✓	✓*
Belgium-de	•	✓
Bulgaria	•	✓
Cyprus	X	✓*
Czech Republic	X	✓
France	✓	✓
Greece	•	✓*
Hungary	✓	✓
Ireland	•	✓
The Netherlands	•	✓
Poland	X	✓
Portugal	X	✓
Slovakia	X	✓
Switzerland	•	✓*

**Belgium:* 2½ years and above; *Cyprus, Greece and Switzerland*: 4 years and above
Source: SEEPRO-3 country reports, in: Oberhuemer/Schreyer 2024b

The tables indicate that ECEC curricula have been issued in *all* the 33 SEEPRO-3 countries for work with children from 3 years up to primary school entry. In most cases they represent a mandatory framework and are anchored in legislation. However, specified guidelines for working with children under 3 years of age remain less regulated, if they exist at all. Also, those that do exist are rarely legally binding. As a rule, ECEC professionals are free to choose the didactic approaches and materials they use.

4.3.2   Curricular content

In terms of curricular content, certain core areas of learning and development are reiterated across countries. These include language/literacy and communication; personal and social development; creativity; mathematics and science; music and movement; physical development. Otherwise, the range of curricular content is broad. An emphasis on play as a basic learning activity is emphasised in many cases, particularly in frameworks for work with the youngest age group.

Digital education

Digital devices are part of children's everyday life. However, *digital education* does not have the same prominence in ECEC curricular frameworks and is not systematically included as a learning area in all countries.

In the countries with a *unitary* ECEC system, it is mentioned in all country curricula with the exception of *Estonia*. Although access to the internet has been considered a 'human right' in Estonia since 2000 and digital literacy is a key competence in the Lifelong Learning Strategy 2020, it is not mentioned in the ECEC curriculum. In *Ukraine*, digital education is included in the curriculum as a new learning area.

In the *part-integrated* ECEC systems, digital education is mostly included, although in some countries subsumed under an existing area such as 'language' or 'technologies'. Among the *UK* nations, no reference is made to ICT (information and communication technologies) or digital education, except in *Northern Ireland*. In *Germany*, digital education has little prominence in the federal state curricula. It is only mentioned in four of them – Hamburg, Mecklenburg-Vorpommern, North Rhine-Westphalia and Thuringia –, in some cases through a separately defined learning area. In *Austria*, specific reference is made to the age-appropriate, critical and creative use of digital technologies for children from the age of 3, which should be limited to 30 minutes per day and should only take place when accompanied by a specialist.

Digital education is explicitly mentioned in the curricular frameworks of seven of the 13 countries with a *bi-sectoral* ECEC system (*Bulgaria, Cyprus, France, Greece, Ireland, Portugal, Slovakia*). In the case of *Portugal*, it is included in 'Language and communication'. In *Switzerland*, digital education is included in the pre-primary curricula for 4 and 5 year-olds, but not in the Orientation Framework for ECEC for the younger age group. Although digital education is not included in the curricula for both sectors in *Hungary*, the Hungarian Government's Digital Strategy adopted in 2016 clearly states that knowledge of information technology and digital education needs to be integrated into everyday activities in kindergartens and also emphasises that kindergartens need the appropriate resources for this. Moreover, it is recommended that the training of professionals be adapted and that specialist centres be set up to support the ECEC settings with support needs in this area.

Overall, in the majority of curricular frameworks, no specific detail is offered with regard to the digital skills and competences to be acquired. Instead, rather general possibilities for the use of digital technologies are described, such as reading e-books, playing computer games or using a digital camera. A point often made is that the (age-appropriate) introduction to digital technologies should represent an 'added value' in the children's experiences in the ECEC centre and should not replace real-life experiences, but rather supplement them. An issue that is often mentioned is that ECEC professionals themselves should have the opportunity to further educate themselves in the use of digital media for their own work.

4.4 Evaluation and assessment

Evaluation and monitoring are increasingly being addressed in international studies in the field of early childhood education and care (e.g. OECD 2015; Klinkhammer et al. 2017). They also comprise one of the five pillars of quality development recommended in the European Quality Framework for ECEC (European Commission 2014). In the SEEPRO-3 study, the topics were included, whereby the focus is primarily on institution-based, evaluative assessment procedures and not on monitoring in the sense of a system-related steering procedure (non-evaluative, criteria-led, longitudinal) (cf. DeGEval 2016: 68).

In the research literature, a distinction is made between 'internal evaluation' or 'self-evaluation' and 'external evaluation' (cf. e.g. DeGEval 2016: 66f). *Self-evaluation* is understood as a procedure "…in which the evaluators belong to the same organisation that is responsible for the object of evaluation." In our study, these are predominantly the core professionals and centre leaders, possibly also ECEC counsellors or consultants commissioned by the provider. In contrast, in an *external evaluation*, "...the evaluators do not belong to the organisation responsible for the object of the evaluation (DeGEval 2016: 66)." In our study, such evaluators are usually representatives of educational or administrative authorities, evaluation institutions or the inspectorate of the responsible ministries.

Three categories served as structuring elements in the SEEPRO-3 study:

- *Child-related assessment* in the sense of an ongoing review of children's developmental progress and/or performance – primarily formative, but also summative where appropriate
- *Centre-based self-evaluation*, i.e. assessments by staff and centre leaders of their own work – as a basis for the further development of internal planning and priorities
- *External evaluation*, intended to provide an objective, criteria-led view of the ECEC centre from the outside and carried out by representatives of the supervisory authorities (or on their behalf), usually by education authorities or evaluation institutions.

The criteria for internal and external evaluations include, for example, quality assurance measures such as working conditions, financial and personnel resources and management quality as well as measures to ensure pedagogical and process quality.

Regulations on the mandatory implementation of the three evaluation categories were also analysed, as were the specifications on time intervals.

4.4.1 Child-related assessment

A more detailed analysis across the 33 SEEPRO-3 countries shows that mandatory assessment of children applies mainly in ECEC for the two or three years prior to school entry. This is the case in the *Flemish Community of Belgium*, the *Czech Republic, Estonia, France, Greece, Hungary, Lithuania, Luxembourg, The Netherlands, Poland, Portugal, Romania, Slovakia, Sweden* as well as *England* and *Wales (UK)*.

There are a further seven countries (*Austria, Bulgaria, Croatia, Denmark, Finland, Latvia, Spain*) in which child-related assessment measures are carried out across the entire ECEC phase. Only in three countries (*Hungary, Lithuania, The Netherlands*) is an assessment explicitly mandatory for the under-3s age group.

As a rule, such assessments are carried out by the ECEC staff through observations, written notes or compiling a portfolio of the children's work and are discussed with the parents. In some countries (e.g. *Hungary, Ireland*), tests or screenings are also used. A certificate of 'school readiness' is issued in the *German-speaking Community of Belgium, Bulgaria, Croatia, Estonia* and *Slovakia*, for example, and may be handed over to the primary school on transfer. Language proficiency assessments are obligatory in *Austria* (at least once a year from the age of 3), *Denmark* (for children who do not attend an ECEC centre) and in some federal states for certain age groups in *Germany*.

However, in 11 countries (*Czech Republic, Greece, Ireland, Italy, Norway, Portugal, Russia, Serbia, Slovenia, Sweden, Ukraine*) and in the *German-speaking Community of Belgium* there are no regulations for assessing the developmental progress of children under the age of 3.

In *Bulgaria* and *Romania*, children are assessed at the beginning and end of their time in kindergarten.

4.4.2   Centre-based self-evaluation

Similar trends can also be seen with regard to centre-based self-evaluation. Only in the *French Community of Belgium* and in *The Netherlands* is this also mandatory in centres for under 3 year-olds – compared to a total of 23 countries in which self-evaluation is mandatory in centres for children aged 3 or 4 and above or in ECEC centres for both age groups. Although such evaluations are not mandatory in most centres for under 3 year-olds, it may be recommended that they are carried out (e.g. in *Croatia, Ireland, Portugal*).

The centre leader is usually responsible for supervising the implementation; the evaluation results can also serve as a basis for drawing up a longer-term development plan for the centre (e.g. in *Croatia, Hungary, Latvia, The Netherlands* or in pre-primary classes in *Luxembourg*). Frequent focal points of such centre-based internal evaluation procedures are financial and human resources, management, the learning environment, equipment, teamwork or staff satisfaction. The involvement of parents also plays a role in several countries (e.g. in the *Czech Republic, Denmark, France, Germany*) – as does a comparison of whether the goals of the institution have been achieved or whether the implementation of educational plans or curricula has been successful (e.g. *Croatia, Portugal*). In certain countries, the decision on the use of the results of the self-evaluation lies with the institutions themselves (e.g. in *Denmark, Finland, Sweden*), as does the choice of methods or focal points (e.g. in *Estonia, Ireland, The Netherlands, Romania*).

In some countries, there are no regulations in this regard, such as in ECEC services for under 3 year-olds in the *German-speaking Community of Belgium*, the *Czech Republic, Italy, Malta, Poland*, as well as in ECEC centres for under 4 year-olds in *Greece*. In *Ukraine*, it is reported that there is no tradition of self-evaluation and basically no coherent system for monitoring and evaluation.

4.4.3 External evaluation

Across all types of evaluation, external evaluations of ECEC provision are most frequently mandatory, both in centres for children under 3 years of age (in 12 countries) and in centres for children aged 3 or 4 and above (in 17 countries) as well as in integrated centres for both age groups (in 16 countries). For centres attended by both age groups, this type of evaluation is optional only in *Croatia, Germany* (with the exception of the city state of Berlin), and *Ukraine*.

As a rule, external evaluations are carried out by inspectorates, education authorities or quality agencies. The criteria used for the checks are extremely varied: on the one hand they can include the inspection of safety regulations, buildings, rooms, equipment, food and hygiene. On the other hand, they may include compliance with rules and regulations, e.g. with regard to staffing ratios or the number of children in a group; management quality; setting organisation; educational plans; finances; or staff qualifications. A wide variety of methods are used for the review, from observations, document analyses, questionnaires and checklists to interviews and – invariably – on-site visits. The results are usually recorded in a report, which may also be followed by an assessment certificate or 'quality seal'. In some cases, the results are also communicated to the wider public via the centre website.

Supplementary note: Frequency of evaluation procedures

The frequency with which evaluations are (or should be) carried out varies greatly across countries. Overall, however, it can be stated that *child-related assessments* take place more frequently than centre-based self-evaluations or external evaluations. For example, in the *French Community of Belgium* (for both age groups, although not mandatory), in *Lithuania* (for 6 to 7 year-olds) and in *Malta* (for over 3 year-olds), the results of child-related assessments are discussed with parents twice a year; in *Luxembourg*, formative evaluations take place every three months in the pre-primary classes for 4 and 5 year-olds.

The intervals between *centre-based self-evaluations* vary considerably. In nine countries, it was reported that they take place once a year, even if they are not mandatory: in centres for over 3 year-olds in *Cyprus, Greece, Malta, Poland, Portugal* and *Slovakia;* in centres for both age groups in *Norway, Slovenia* and *Spain*. On the other hand, in *Bulgaria*, centres for over 3 year-olds are only obliged to carry out such a self-evaluation once every five years, in *Luxembourg* and *The Netherlands* every four years; in centres with children up to school age in *Denmark* and *Latvia* every two years.

External evaluations are generally carried out even less frequently: they are mandatory every five years for centres for over 3 year-olds in the *German-speaking Community of Belgium*, in *Hungary* and *Portugal*, as well as for centres for the entire age group up to school entry in *Serbia*. In *Cyprus, Italy* and *Luxembourg*, an external evaluation is generally carried out every three years for centres for over 3 year-olds.

4.5 Inclusion and transitions

4.5.1 Inclusion agendas

Both the UN Convention on the Rights of the Child and the UN Convention on the Rights of Persons with Disabilities (United Nations 1989; 2006) have been ratified by most countries in the world, including the 33 SEEPRO-3 countries.

Since this time, significant progress has also been made in early childhood education and childcare systems towards an inclusive approach. For example, two thirds of the SEEPRO-3 country reports (22) state that children with special educational needs and disabilities (SEND) should attend mainstream ECEC centres 'whenever possible'. Only if adequate support is not possible in regular provision should they attend (separate) support centres. Often specific support groups are set up within mainstream centres with additional special needs staff (e.g. in *Estonia, Slovakia*).

As a rule, the treatment of children with special educational needs and their right to individualised support is regulated by law in national/federal state ECEC or school education legislation. Special needs groups, whether in mainstream settings or in separate centres, are smaller in size compared to regular groups. In 15 country reports (e.g. *France, Hungary, Italy, Portugal, Slovenia*) it is explicitly mentioned that an individual education or development plan is drawn up for each child with special educational needs. In three countries (*Greece, Lithuania, Poland*) the curriculum is adapted accordingly for this group of children and in *Bulgaria* there are state educational standards for inclusive education.

No significant differences can be identified in the country reports with regard to the age groups of children under and over 3 years of age or according to the type of ECEC system in the countries.

A prerequisite for the appropriate support of children with SEND is that the professionals who work with them are sufficiently qualified to do so. In *Austria*, for example, children in integrative kindergarten groups (which include four children with disabilities and 16 children without) are cared for and educated jointly by an Early Childhood Pedagogue whose IPE explicitly includes elements of inclusive education, a Special Needs Pedagogue and two Pedagogical Assistants. In *Finland*, a university-trained Special Needs Teacher is present in inclusive groups – if the respective local authority provides the necessary funding – and also has an advisory role. Since 2024, kindergartens in *Poland* (with 41 to 50 children) have been entitled to an additional special needs specialist; larger kindergartens (with 51–100 children or more) are entitled to an additional one-and-a-half or two special needs specialists (Eurydice 2024).

State or municipal funding is essential to support ECEC centres in purchasing or adapting materials, equipment or premises according to the children's needs, ensuring that a high quality education is guaranteed for children with SEND. In the *Flemish Community of Belgium*, for example, more hours or funding are granted if children require additional support. In *Croatia*, children with special needs can attend the compulsory pre-primary programme for two years instead of one, and municipal facilities can apply for additional funding for more staff. In *Romania*, a child may be looked after by an extra support specialist; in addition, a national centre for inclusive education with its own budget was established in 2022. In the *Czech Republic*, kindergarten staff are supported through relevant CPD programmes.

Statistical figures on the proportion of children in inclusive/integrative groups or in special needs centres are not available in all country reports. The proportion of children attending separate support centres across the countries – as far as is known – is usually around 1% of the age group.

In *Italy*, 2.4% of children with disabilities were enrolled in pre-primary centres (3–5 years) in 2021, 2.8% in public and 1.2% in private institutions (ISTAT 2023). These *scuole dell'infanzia* usually employ a Special Needs Teacher. In the non-formal sector in *Luxembourg*, only 1% of children with disabilities attend a separate institution. Moreover, nine competence centres were established at national level in 2018 which support inclusive settings and also offer monitoring. In *Norway*, children who cannot benefit sufficiently from mainstream ECEC centres are entitled to receive special support; in 2022, this was the case for 2.1% of children in municipal kindergartens and 1.5% in private kindergartens (Statistics Norway 2023, own calculations). In *Portugal*, support for under 6 year-olds with special needs is regulated by the national intervention system, as well as through local resource centres and collaboration with experts. Only 1% of children who cannot be supported in mainstream institutions attend support centres. In *Poland*, 6% of kindergartens for 3 to 6 year-olds had inclusive groups in 2023/24 (Eurydice 2024, 12.1). In 2022/23, 9% of all children in kindergarten attended a separate special kindergarten; 0.6% of under 3 year-olds with disabilities attended mainstream facilities (GUS 2023a). More than half of these settings (59.5%) have been adapted to the needs of children with disabilities (GUS 2023b, 1, 3, own calculation). In 2021/22 in *Spain*, 1.3% of children in the 1st cycle (0–2) and 3.2% in the 2nd

cycle (3–5) had special educational needs (Spanish Ministry of Education and Vocational Training 2023: 9).

4.5.2   Transitions to and from ECEC settings

Transitions – especially from ECEC to primary school, but also from home to ECEC setting or from one centre to another – tend to be seen as a challenge for both children and professionals. The report from *Switzerland* also highlights the problem of 'double transitions', when children move from a childcare centre (0–3 years) to pre-primary education (4–5 years) while additionally attending an afternoon childcare facility that supplements their time in school. Generally speaking, professionals from the participating settings are faced with the challenge of creating coherence and continuity.

In the following, some reported examples of transition measures are listed, primarily related to the transition from ECEC centre to primary school:

- Specifying required professional competences needed for successfully planning transition issues (e.g. *Bulgaria, Croatia, Germany, Estonia, Malta, Portugal, Slovakia, Switzerland, United Kingdom*)
- Organising regular consultations both at the steering level (between representatives of the relevant ministries and authorities) and at the setting level (between ECEC centre leaders and school heads, between ECEC staff and school teachers), as reported for *Belgium, Cyprus, France, Greece, The Netherlands* and *Ukraine*
- Including the topic of transitions in the ECEC curricular frameworks (e.g. *Denmark, Estonia, France, Luxembourg, Norway*)
- Coordinating the framework curricula of ECEC centres and schools more closely (e.g. *Finland, Portugal, Slovenia*)
- Organising projects to improve transition planning (e.g. *Belgium, Italy, Slovenia, Spain*)
- Providing CPD and training events for professionals on the topic of 'transitions' (e.g. *France, Italy, Slovenia, Spain*)
- Enhancing certain types of institutionalised transition groups, such as the transition classes (*classes passerelles*) for 2 year-olds in the French *écoles maternelles*, the bridge classes (*sezioni primavera*) in the *scuole dell'infanzia* in *Italy*, the integration of pre-primary classes/kindergartens into primary schools in *Switzerland*. The various kinds of compulsory pre-primary programmes in 21 countries also belong to this category (see chapter 4.1.2).

In some countries, a written notification of the child's assessed 'school readiness' is handed over (only with the parents' consent) to the primary school (e.g. *Bulgaria, Croatia, Estonia, Hungary, Lithuania, Poland, Slovakia, UK-England* and *UK-Scotland*). In *Austria*, the primary school receives a mandatory handover sheet regarding the language assessment carried out in the ECEC centre. Similarly, in *Romania*, the child's level of development is recorded in writing for the transition to primary school.

4.6 Working parents, parenting leave and post-leave entitlement to ECEC

4.6.1 Parental employment[6]

Contextualising the ECEC workforce in a broader sense also includes taking into account relevant social and family policy developments that affect the parents of children in ECEC centres: for example, the employment rates of mothers and fathers as well as family support options that are open to them, especially during the first year or so following the child's birth. Moreover, the question arises at the end of parenting leave as to whether parents are entitled to a place in an ECEC setting with flexible opening hours and fair cost structures, particularly for low-income parents.

During the period between 2010 and 2022, the employment of mothers with children under 6 years of age increased in all but four of the 33 SEEPRO-3 countries (*Cyprus, Czech Republic, Denmark* and *Romania*), in some cases significantly. In five countries, the increase was between 36 (*Hungary*) and 21 percentage points (*Estonia*), in 12 countries between 18 (*Slovenia*) and 6 percentage points (*Portugal*) and in 11 countries between 5% (*Latvia*) and 1% (*Italy*). The highest increase (albeit not as high as for mothers) in working fathers from 2010 to 2022 can be seen in *Lithuania* at 15%; in five other countries employment increased between 14 (*Czech Republic*) and 10 percentage points (*Ireland*), in seven countries between 10% (*Estonia*) and 5% (*Bulgaria*) and in eight countries between 4% (*Sweden*) and 0.6% (*France*).

In 2022, however, the shares of working fathers in the SEEPRO-3 countries (no data for Russia and Ukraine) are still significantly higher than those of mothers: the highest share is found in *Switzerland* at 95.3%, the lowest in *Serbia* at 78.5%. This contrasts with shares of 82.9% for mothers in *Norway* and 42.5% in the *Czech Republic*. The smallest difference between the employment of mothers and fathers can be observed in *Luxembourg*, where the shares differ by only 8.5%; the largest difference is to be found in the *Czech Republic* at 51.5%. One reason for these differences, some of which are considerable,

---

6 Data reported in this section are based on the SEEPRO-3 Key Contextual Data synopses, in: Oberhuemer/Schreyer 2024b.

could be that the traditional distribution of roles in the family and a still predominantly maternalistic view of bringing up young children in the home continue to be more strongly embedded in some countries than in others.

4.6.2 Parenting leave[7]

In almost all SEEPRO-3 countries, *maternity leave* (or at least a proportionate period) is legally binding (except in *Norway, Portugal* and *Sweden*). Overall it is remunerated at a relatively high level (more than 66% of income, sometimes with a cap). In *Ireland*, however, maternity leave is unpaid, and in the *UK* only with a lower payment for less than half of the time. In *Bulgaria, Croatia, Greece* (private sector) and the *Czech Republic*, parts of the leave can also be transferred to the father.

The duration of maternity leave varies considerably: from one year in *Bulgaria* to just two weeks in *Sweden*; in the latter case, this is immediately followed by around eight months of parental leave. In most SEEPRO-3 countries (19), maternity leave lasts between ten weeks and six months.

As a rule, maternity leave is followed by a period of state-subsidised *parental leave*. Only in *Switzerland* is this kind of leave not available, unless the employer offers such a measure. In all other SEEPRO-3 countries, parental leave is offered either as a family or individual entitlement, the duration of which and, where applicable, the remuneration and conditions of entitlement vary greatly.

For example, parenting leave in *Portugal* lasts three months, while parents in the *Czech Republic, Estonia, Hungary, Lithuania, Russia, Slovakia, Spain* and *Ukraine* are entitled to three years. The necessary condition for taking parental leave is usually a certain period of previous employment and/or payment into a social insurance scheme. In most countries, parental leave or at a least part of it is remunerated according to certain conditions. In *Ireland, Malta, Portugal, Spain* (where only social security contributions continue to be paid) no remuneration is paid and parents only have the option of taking time off work. In the *United Kingdom*, 14 months of shared parental leave are available, of which only six weeks are well paid (Moss/Mitchell 2024).

Any payment can be subject to a wide variety of conditions: often an income-related share is paid (e.g. in *Denmark, Germany, Luxembourg*); in some countries, however, parents also receive their full previous salary – at least for part of the parental leave – such as in *Estonia* (for 475 days out of a total of three years), in *Croatia*, in *Lithuania* (two months per parent out of a total of three years), in *Norway*, in *Poland* (20 weeks out of 41 weeks), in *Serbia* and in *Slovenia*.

---

7 The main source orientation for the information in this and the following section was: International Network on Leave Policies & Research 2023a.

In most countries, it is possible for both parents to take parental leave, or parts of it, at the same time. In addition, some countries offer further opportunities to take additional time off and/or receive financial support. In *Belgium*, for example, employees have the right to take 20 days of 'birth leave' in the four months following the child's birth, three of which are fully paid and the remainder at 82% of salary. After the end of parental leave (160 days), parents in *Finland* can take 'home care time' until the child's 3rd birthday, which is remunerated with a lump sum of approx. €378/month. Working parents of children under the age of 3 in *Slovakia* can receive a 'childcare allowance': €80/month for care in a kindergarten attached to a school, €280 for care in other public facilities and €41 for other people looking after the child.

4.6.3 Post-leave entitlement to ECEC

Enrolment in an ECEC setting can be seen as a measure that enables parents to return to work relatively quickly after leave arrangements and that also offers children opportunities to learn, play and socialise with their peers. If the leave modalities are not adequately designed to meet the needs of parents, there may be a (sometimes significant) gap between the end of parenting leave and entitlement to a place in ECEC provision (see also International Network on Leave Policies & Research 2023b).

In countries with *unitary* ECEC systems in particular (with the exception of *Croatia* and *Lithuania*, where there is no legal entitlement to a place in an ECEC centre for children under the age of 3), it is generally possible to enrol a child in an ECEC setting immediately after the end of parenting leave.

This is also possible in most countries with a *part-integrated* ECEC system. The exceptions here are *Italy* and *Serbia* (no entitlement for under 3 year-olds) as well as *Austria* and the *United Kingdom*, where the gap between the end of parenting leave and entitlement to a place in an ECEC setting at the age of three or just under two is considerable. However, it must also be borne in mind that in some countries (e.g. *Germany, Luxembourg, Romania, Russia*), an entitlement to a place in an ECEC setting directly after the end of parenting leave is envisaged, but cannot always be materialised due to a lack of places.

In eight of the 13 countries with a *bi-sectoral* system, there are clear gaps between the end of parental leave and the entitlement to attend an ECEC centre, ranging from 7.3 months (*Ireland*) to 50 months (*Cyprus*). Only in four of the countries is ECEC entitlement directly linked to the end of parental leave (*Czech Republic, France, Hungary, Poland*).

Part II

The ECEC workforce

5 Key pedagogical and specialist support staff

This chapter focuses both on the core pedagogical staff working on a regular basis in early childhood education and care centre-based settings and on the specialist staff supporting them. It concludes with an overview of the composition of staff in ECEC settings according to qualification and gender.

Key pedagogical staff include the group-leading *core practitioners* (sometimes referred to as core pedagogues or core professionals), ECEC *centre leaders* and *co-working assistants*. Key specialist support staff refers to a variety of ECEC counselling, advisory and inspection staff as well as diverse special needs and other specialists who may work directly in the centre but are more often employed by external services.

5.1 Core practitioners: minimum qualification requirements and professional profiles

5.1.1 Minimum qualification requirement for working as a core practitioner

Most core professionals in the 33 SEEPRO-3 countries follow a higher education course of study leading to a Bachelor's degree or equivalent (ISCED 6) at a university or university of applied sciences.

In the *unitary* ECEC systems, this is the case for all countries: *Croatia, Denmark, Estonia, Finland, Latvia[8], Lithuania, Norway, Slovenia, Sweden* and *Ukraine*.

Among the *part-integrated* ECEC systems, *Germany* represents a special case among the staff qualified at ISCED level 6. Here, most Early Childhood Educators are prepared for the profession at a tertiary level vocational college specialising in social pedagogy, as a rule with a substantial but not exclusive focus on early childhood education and care. Only a small minority of ECEC staff (almost 6% in 2023) are educated at universities or universities of applied sciences.

Cyprus and *Greece* present an exception among the 13 countries with *bi-sectoral* ECEC systems. While the core practitioners both in the childcare sector and in the education sector have an ISCED level 6 qualification, those working in nurseries study at a university of applied sciences whereas those

---

8 In *Latvia* it is also still possible to work as core practitioner in an ECEC institution with an ISCED 5 qualification.

working in kindergartens for 4 and 5 year-olds attend a four-year specialist course at a university.

In countries with a minimum qualification requirement lower than the ISCED 6 classification for core practitioners, even for those working with children above the age of 3 (*Austria, Czech Republic, Russia, Slovakia*), initial professional education takes place at various kinds of vocational education institutions (specialist and non-specialist) at the upper secondary and post-secondary, non-tertiary levels or, in the case of *Austria*, at short-cycle tertiary level.

Findings of previous SEEPRO studies suggest that changes in the minimum formal requirements for taking up work as a core practitioner in early childhood settings has changed only in a few cases over the past 15 years.

The following three tables, ordered according to ECEC system type, show the requirements valid in 2010 and in 2024. Also indicated is the institution type currently responsible for initial professional education. The 2010 requirements (which were classified according to ISCED 1997) are shown in the correspondence to the current ISCED 2011 levels (UNESCO 2012, Section 10). What were formerly ISCED 5A or 5B qualifications under ISCED 1997 are now classified as ISCED 5, 6 or 7, according to the specific level of vocational or academic education.

In the *unitary* ECEC systems (Table 11) the required minimum qualification for working as a core practitioner has remained consistently at a high level. Both in 2010 and in 2024 this was a Bachelor's degree (ISCED 6) awarded by a university or other higher education institution.

Table 11

Core practitioners: minimum qualification requirements in unitary ECEC systems, 2010 and 2024

Country	2010 ISCED 1997	2024 ISCED 2011	IPE institutions 2024
Croatia 0–5	***	ISCED 6 Bachelor	University
Denmark 0–5	ISCED 5A Bachelor (since 2001)	ISCED 6 Bachelor	University College
Estonia 0–6	ISCED 5A Bachelor (since 2000)	ISCED 6 Bachelor	University
Finland 0–6	ISCED 5A Bachelor (since 1995)	ISCED 6 Bachelor	University* or University of applied sciences**
Latvia 0–6	ISCED 5A/B Bachelor (since 1994)	ISCED 5/6 Bachelor	University affiliated professional/higher education

Country	2010 ISCED 1997	2024 ISCED 2011	IPE institutions 2024
Lithuania 0–6	ISCED 5A/B Bachelor (since 2006)	ISCED 6 Bachelor	University or other Higher Education Institution (HEI)
Norway 0–5	***	ISCED 6 Bachelor	University or University College
Slovenia 0–5	ISCED 5A Bachelor (since 1995)	ISCED 6 Bachelor	University
Sweden 0–5	ISCED 5A Bachelor (since 2001)	ISCED 6 Bachelor	University or University College
Ukraine 0–6	***	ISCED 6 Bachelor	University

*Teacher in ECEC **Social Pedagogue in ECEC *** Not part of the SEEPRO study published in 2010
Sources: Oberhuemer/Schreyer/Neuman 2010; SEEPRO-3 country reports in: Oberhuemer/Schreyer 2024b

Among the *part-integrated* ECEC systems (Table 12), an upgrading has taken place in *Austria, Italy* and *Malta*. Particularly in *Italy*, a significantly higher formal level of qualification is now required for work with under 3 year-olds (ISCED 6) than was the case in 2010 (ISCED 3). This took place within the fundamental reform of the Italian ECEC system initiated in 2017 to promote the change from a bi-sectoral to a unitary system. In *Austria*, the post-secondary qualifying route has now been upgraded to an ISCED 5 award (short-cycle tertiary education), and in *Malta*, the core practitioners who work in kindergarten centres 3–4 are now classified at ISCED 5 level, which represents an upgrading compared with the situation in 2010 but still means that it is one of the four countries without a Bachelor's degree requirement for the work with over 3 year-olds.

Table 12
Core practitioners: minimum qualification requirements in part-integrated ECEC systems, 2010 and 2024

Country	2010 ISCED 1997	2024 ISCED 2011	IPE institutions 2024
Austria 0–5	ISCED 4A	Professional diploma ↗ ISCED 5	Tertiary level college specialising in early childhood pedagogy
Germany 0–5	ISCED 5B	State certificate* ISCED 6 Bachelor equivalent	Tertiary level college specialising in social pedagogy

Country	2010 ISCED 1997	2024 ISCED 2011	IPE institutions 2024
Italy			
0–2	ISCED 3A	↗ ISCED 6 Bachelor	University
3–5	ISCED 5A Bachelor equivalent	↗ ISCED 7 Master equiv.	
Luxembourg			
0–3	ISCED 4A	ISCED 4	Post-secondary vocational
4–5	ISCED 5A Bachelor	ISCED 6 Bachelor	University
Malta			
0–2	ISCED 3B/C	↗ ISCED 4	Post-secondary vocational
3–4	ISCED 3B/C	↗ ISCED 5	
Romania			
0–2	ISCED 4A	ISCED 4	Post-secondary vocational
3–5	ISCED 5A Bachelor	ISCED 6 Bachelor	University
Russia			
0–2	***	ISCED 4	Post-secondary vocational
3–6		ISCED 4**	college specialising in pedagogy
Serbia			
0–2	***	ISCED 3	Upper secondary vocational
3–6		ISCED 6 Bachelor	University
Spain			
0–2	ISCED 4A/B	ISCED 4	Post-secondary vocational
3–5	ISCED 5A Bachelor	ISCED 6 Bachelor	University
UK 0–4	Setting-specific, ranging from ISCED 3 to ISCED 6	Setting-specific, ranging from ISCED 3 to ISCED 6 across nations	Ranging from upper secondary vocational to University

*In some federal states a Bachelor (professional) is awarded.
** Estimated classification, since ISCED not widely used in Russia
*** Not part of the SEEPRO study published in 2010.
Sources: Oberhuemer/Schreyer/Neuman 2010; SEEPRO-3 country reports in: Oberhuemer/Schreyer 2024b

For staff working in the education sectors of the *bi-sectoral* systems (Table 13), a significant upgrading has taken place in *France, Poland and Portugal*, which places the early childhood professionals on a par with Primary School Teachers. In these countries (as is also the case in Italy), a Master's degree is now the required minimum qualification for working with children from the age of 3 years up to primary school entry, i.e. a qualification at ISCED level 7. In *Belgium* and *Ireland*, for group leaders in the childcare and non-primary sectors, respectively, the minimum qualification requirement has been raised to ISCED level 4.

Table 13
Core practitioners: minimum qualification requirements in bi-sectoral ECEC systems, 2010 and 2024

Country	2010 – ISCED 1997	2024 – ISCED 2011	IPE institutions 2024
Belgium			
0–2	ISCED 3B	↗ ISCED 4	Post-secondary vocational
3–5	ISCED 5B Bachelor	ISCED 6 Bachelor	University
Bulgaria			
0–2	ISCED 5A/B Bachelor	ISCED 6 Bachelor	University
3–6	ISCED 5A/B Bachelor	ISCED 6 Bachelor	
Cyprus			
0–3	ISCED 5A/B	ISCED 6 Bachelor	University of applied sciences
4–5	ISCED 5A Bachelor	ISCED 6 Bachelor	University
Czech Rep.			
0–2	ISCED 3A	ISCED 3	Upper secondary vocational
3–5	ISCED 3A	ISCED 3*	
France			
0–2	ISCED 3	ISCED 3	Upper secondary vocational
3–5	ISCED 5A Bachelor	↗ ISCED 7 Master equiv.	University-affiliated HEI
Greece			
0–3	ISCED 5A/B	ISCED 6 Bachelor	University of applied sciences
4–5	ISCED 5A Bachelor	ISCED 6 Bachelor	University
Hungary			
0–2	ISCED 4A/B	ISCED 4*	Post-secondary vocational
3–5	ISCED 5B Bachelor	↗ ISCED 6 Bachelor	University
Ireland			
0–3	ISCED 3A/C	↗ ISCED 4	Post-secondary vocational
4–5	ISCED 5A/B Bachelor	ISCED 6 Bachelor	University
The Netherlands			
0–3	ISCED 3B	ISCED 3	Upper secondary vocational
4–5	ISCED 5A Bachelor	ISCED 6 Bachelor	Specialist Pedagogical Academy (4 years) or University (5 years)
Poland			
0–2	ISCED 3	ISCED 3	Upper secondary vocational
3–6	ISCED 5A/B Bachelor	↗ ISCED 7 Master	University
Portugal			
0–2	ISCED 5A/B Bachelor	↗ ISCED 7 Master	University
3–5	ISCED 5A/B Bachelor	↗ ISCED 7 Master	
Slovakia			
0–2	ISCED n/a	ISCED 3	Upper secondary vocational
3–5	ISCED 3/4	ISCED 3/4	

Country	2010 – ISCED 1997	2024 – ISCED 2011	IPE institutions 2024
Switzerland			
0–3	**	ISCED 3	Upper secondary vocational
4–5		ISCED 6 Bachelor	University of applied sciences

Czech Republic: approx. 24% of the workforce in kindergartens 2–6 have a Bachelor's degree or higher (2020) – see Loudová Stralczynská 2024; *Hungary:* 25% of the workforce in nurseries 0–2 have a Bachelor's degree or higher (2021/22) – see Korintus 2024
** Not part of the SEEPRO study published in 2010
Sources: Oberhuemer/Schreyer/Neuman 2010; SEEPRO-3 country reports in: Oberhuemer/Schreyer 2024b

Supplementary note: Working hours of core practitioners

In order to be able to better assess how much time the core pedagogues spend in the centres and with the children, some information on the total amount of working hours per week and the proportion of working time without direct contact with the children ('non-contact hours') is presented here.

– Full time or part time?

In the 33 SEEPRO-3 countries, the majority of core practitioners work on a full-time basis. The number of required hours for a full-time post varies across countries and may also vary between providers within the same country. 'Full time' means a 40-hour week in *Austria, Bulgaria, Croatia,* the *Czech Republic, Hungary, Latvia, Romania, Serbia, Slovenia* and *Sweden*. Non-contact hours are included in this total and vary across countries (see below). Otherwise, a full working week may amount to between 36 hours (*Lithuania, Russia*) and 38.5 hours (*Germany*).

In countries in which pre-primary education is located within the school system (e.g. *Belgium* or *Malta*), the full-time working hours of professionals working with over 3 year-olds are comparable to the teaching hours in primary school and amount to between 25 and 28 hours per week. In some cases, it was reported that the weekly hours of employment for those working with very young children are longer than those working with older children, e.g. in *Belgium* (38 vs. 26 hours per week) or in *Latvia* (40 vs. 30 hours). In *Italy*, the number of full-time working hours in a pre-primary school (*scuola dell'infanzia*) for 3 to under 6 year-olds varies between providers and can range from 25 hours (excluding non-contact time) in public settings and 36 hours in municipal-run provision to between 31 and 38 hours in private pre-primary schools.

However, the proportion of full-time employees in the workforce varies considerably across countries. While in ten countries – *Flemish Community of Belgium, Bulgaria, Croatia, Cyprus, Estonia, Finland, France, Hungary, Serbia* and *Slovenia* – more than 80% of professionals are employed full time, in the *French Community of Belgium* and in *Norway* this is the case for only around two thirds of core practitioners.

In six of the SEEPRO-3 countries, part-time work predominates: in *Austria* (roughly 60%), *Belgium – German-speaking Community* (just over half), *Denmark* (60%), *Germany* (around 66%) and in *Lithuania* (over 65%). In *Switzerland*, no nation-wide statistics are available on full-time and part-time employment in the childcare sector 0–3. In pre-primary education settings, nearly 77% of Kindergarten Teachers in public schools and just over 19% in private schools work less than 50% of a full-time position (Swiss Federal Statistical Office 2023).

– Non-contact time

Generally speaking, the number of hours that core practitioners are allocated for planning, preparation work, team consultations, cooperation with parents, community networking and other activities relevant to work in an ECEC setting varies according to the setting provider and (in *bi-sectoral* and some *part-integrated* ECEC systems) on the sector in which they are employed.

In nine of the SEEPRO-3 countries – *Belgium, Denmark, Estonia, France, Russia, Sweden, Switzerland, Ukraine* and the *UK* – it was reported that there are no official regulations regarding time away from direct work with the children. In the *French Community of Belgium, Switzerland* and the *UK*, this only applies to the predominantly privately owned childcare settings.

In *Austria* and *Germany*, regulations for non-contact time vary from federal state to federal state. In the nine federal states of *Austria* this can range from no specified non-contact time to ten hours per week. In *Germany*, there are no regulations in two of the 16 federal states (Bremen, Hamburg), whereas in Baden-Wuerttemberg there is a clear specification of at least ten hours per group/week. In the predominantly private childcare sectors for under 3 year-olds in the *Czech Republic*, *Malta* and *Poland*, regulations differ among providers. In *Lithuania*, time allocation for non-contact work depends on the organisational model of the respective municipality, i.e. is also here a provider responsibility.

Overall, the number of hours allocated for activities without direct contact with children is very variable. They may range from one hour per week in the non-primary sector in *Ireland* and the childcare sector in *The Netherlands* to 18 hours/week for ECEC professionals working with 6 year-olds in the compulsory kindergarten year in *Poland*.

5.1.2 Professional profiles: definitions and classifications

According to country-specific traditions, occupational job titles in the early childhood field may vary, but in general the main terms chosen for those in charge of a group or class of children are 'teachers', 'educators' or 'pedagogues'. However, if we look more closely at the qualification routes and the types of early childhood setting in which these core practitioners work, then a more differentiated description is needed. Throughout our publications on the early childhood workforce, we have identified six different professional profiles for the core practitioners (see Box 1).[9]

Box 1:
ECEC core professional profiles

1. Early Childhood Pedagogy Professional Specialist focus on the years before entering primary school (0–6/7 years)	Austria 0–5, Croatia 0–5, Denmark 0–5*, Estonia 0–6, Finland 0–6**, Ireland 0–4/5, Latvia 0–6, Lithuania 0–6, Norway 0–6, Portugal 0–5, Slovenia 0–5, Spain 0–5, Sweden 0–6, Ukraine 0–6
2. Pre-primary Education Professional Exclusive pre-primary focus	Belgium 2½–5, Czech Republic 3–5, Cyprus 4–5, Greece 4–5, Hungary 3–5, Malta 3–4, Russia 2–6, Serbia 3–6, Slovakia 3–5, Switzerland 4–5
3. Pre-primary and Primary Education Professional Focus on pre-primary and primary education (3/4–10/11 years)	Bulgaria 3–6, France 3–5, Ireland 4–5, Italy 3–5, Luxembourg (formal) 4–5, The Netherlands 4–5, Poland 3–6, Romania 3–5, Switzerland 4–5
4. Infant-Toddler Professional Exclusive focus on nursery provision	Cyprus 0–2, Hungary 0–2, Malta 0–2, The Netherlands 0–3, Spain 0–2, Russia 0–2
5. Social and Childhood Pedagogy Professional Mainly broad focus, including ECEC and beyond (usually 0–12 years, but in some cases including young adults)	Finland 0–6**, Germany 0–5, Italy 0–2, Luxembourg (non-formal) 0–3, Switzerland 0–3
6. Social Care/Health Care Professional In some cases, early childhood focus, in others a broader focus, including adults	Belgium 0–2, Bulgaria 0–2, France 0–2, Poland 0–2, Serbia 0–2, Slovakia 0–2

*Up to 2014: Social and Childhood Pedagogy Professional
** In Finland 0–6, legislation specifies two types of core professionals, one with an Early Childhood Pedagogy profile, the other with a Social and Childhood Pedagogy profile.
Source: Own presentation

---

9 In the SEEPRO-3 country reports we did not include the Infant-Toddler Professional, but when reviewing all reports at the end of the project, this category was clearly confirmed.

Just for two countries, it was not possible to make such a classification:

- In the *UK* (*England, Wales, Scotland, Northern Ireland*), job titles and qualification requirements are so highly variable, particularly in the private, voluntary and independent sectors of the four nations, that there is no one overall descriptor which would fit across sectors and nations.
- In the childcare sector of the *Czech Republic*, legislation specifies 13 profiles for core staff working in the 'Children's Groups' (0–4/6) established in 2014, ranging from a Caregiver (ISCED 3) to a Primary School Teacher (ISCED 7). Again, no one category can be used to describe the 'core practitioner'.

5.2 Centre leaders in ECEC

In a context of increasingly differentiated expectations and demands on early childhood education and care services, research in various countries has focused more strongly on the role of Centre Leaders in these settings in recent years (Heikka/Hujala 2013; Lunneblad/Garvis 2017; Nicholson et al. 2020; Sakr/O'Sullivan 2022). According to country-specific traditions, systems and settings, these leaders may be called, for example, 'Preschool Principal', 'Kindergarten Director', 'Pedagogical Leader', 'School Head'. There is no core definition of an ECEC Centre Leader, since the range of roles and responsibilities is strongly linked to the type of setting. A Centre Leader may be, for example:

- Head of a one-group kindergarten 3–5 (e.g. *Slovakia*)
- Leader of a mixed-age 0–5 setting (e.g. *Germany, Norway, Slovenia*)
- Head of an ECEC centre 0–5 with several units in different locations and up to 500 children (e.g. *Croatia*)
- Head of a primary school with pre-primary provision (e.g. *Belgium, France, Greece, Malta, The Netherlands, Switzerland*)
- Principal/director of more than one ECEC setting (e.g. *Denmark, Sweden*).

Moreover, leadership profiles may differ considerably across provider types within different nations of one country, as in the case of the *United Kingdom* with its highly diverse provider landscape including private independent, private charitable, social enterprise and state-maintained provision.

5.2.1 *Understandings of leadership*

Approaches towards leadership and management are described in a number of ways in the research literature. These include distributed, collective, dialogical, participatory and team-oriented leadership models. Research on contemporary theoretical conceptualisations presents an understanding of leadership in ECEC as multi-perspective, complex, socially constructed and transformational, clearly moving away from a modernistically hierarchical and linear approach (cf. Nicholson/Maniates 2016). At the core is an understanding that implies shaping the ECEC work environment as a professional learning community for teams – through forms of internal and external assessment, through self, team and management evaluation. For the Centre Leader, this implies needing to learn how to deal with the complexities and contradictions of ECEC leadership and management.

Some of the SEEPRO reports explicitly refer to a hierarchical approach towards leadership within ECEC centres, where management posts tend to be organised in a vertically ranked order (e.g. Director, Deputy Director, Senior Teacher, Senior Methodologist, and so on). The report from *Denmark*, on the other hand, describes leadership structures as "…predominantly collective, based on dialogue and with a flat leadership structure (Koch/Jensen 2024: 387)." Others, such as those from *Finland* and *Ireland*, referred to practising or developing a distributed leadership model. A theoretical research project in *Lithuania* (Dambrauskiene/Liukineviciene 2018) suggests that the current context in the education system is favourable for developing the idea of distributed leadership, but that empirical research needs to follow.

5.2.2 Job requirements

Most ECEC sectors require a certain number of years' *work experience* before taking up a leadership post. The specification may range from 1 year (e.g. *Malta* 0–2, *Lithuania* 0–6) to 8 years in *Serbian* kindergartens 3–5 or at least 12 years for the Principals of large kindergartens/pre-primary schools for 4 and 5 year-olds in *Greece*.

A burning question for those working as Centre Leaders is whether or not they are required to *work with children* alongside their leadership and managerial tasks. The findings of the SEEPRO-3 study showed that this was not the case in most of the ten unitary ECEC systems, although in *Sweden* 0–5, considerable variations between providers were reported: Whereas the greater majority of Principals working in or across public preschools do not spend time in the classroom, nearly two-thirds of those in private settings do. In the other system types the findings were more mixed. In *Germany* 0–5, for example, roughly half of Centre Leaders work with children alongside their leadership tasks, whereas in the non-formal sector of *Luxembourg* they usually do not. In *Spain* 0–5, Early Childhood Teachers are mostly expected to work with children, but their headship duties are included within their teaching hours, i.e. their teaching load is reduced, although the specified number of hours may differ across the Autonomous Communities. This contrasts with the situation in *Greece* 4–5, where the Kindergarten Teachers have full responsibility for a group of children alongside their management and supervisory tasks, with no kind of administrative support and only a modest salary bonus.

In terms of the *formal qualifications* for a leadership post, it is mostly the case – across countries and systems – that no additional basic qualification is required beyond that for core practitioners. At the same time, some countries set higher formal standards. In *Finland* and *Ukraine* 0–6, for example, a Master's degree (ISCED 7) is required instead of a Bachelor's degree. In the childcare settings of *Malta* and *France*, a higher formal qualification is also needed for a leadership post (*Malta*: ISCED 5 instead of 4; *France*: ISCED 6 instead of 3). In the four nations of the *UK*, too, leaders in the private, voluntary and independent sectors are required to have an ISCED 5 or 6 level qualification, whereas core practitioners mostly have ISCED 3 or 4 level certificates or diplomas. Overall, it can be said that Centre Leaders in the ten *unitary* systems have an ISCED level 6 or 7 qualification, whereas in other system types the minimum formal requirements for setting leaders may range from ISCED 3 or 4 to ISCED 6 or 7.

Although it is uncommon for the basic formal qualification to be raised for a leadership post, a number of countries do require *a specific leadership qualification* either before taking up the post or during the first few years of working as a Centre Leader. In the ten *unitary* systems, only *Slovenia* and *Sweden* have such requirements.

– In *Slovenia* 0–5, a leadership course has to be taken either before taking up the post or within one year of starting. Six modules include the following: Organisational theory and leadership, change management; planning and decision-making; finances; personnel management; leadership strategies for learning, assessment, monitor and professional development; legislation in education. However, the course is not targeted specifically at ECEC professionals, but is conceptualised for all those working in educational institutions.
– In *Sweden* 0–5, a university course has been introduced (30 ECTS credits), which Centre Leaders are expected to start within two years of taking up the appointment and complete within five years.

Within the other system types, a pre-post qualification requirement is more common, particularly in the educator sectors of the *bi-sectoral* systems (but rarely in the childcare sectors). This is the case, for example, in the *Czech Republic* 3–5, *France* 2–5, *Hungary* 3–5, *Slovakia* 3–5 and *Switzerland* 4–5. However, only the courses offered in the *Czech Republic* and *Hungary* are specifically focused on work in kindergartens. As in *Slovenia*, they are otherwise more broadly addressed at all specialists working in the education system. An interesting example was reported from *Spain* 0–5: elaborate procedures are in place for selecting the head of an ECEC setting. For example, applicants are required to present a management concept during their interview. The selection is carried out by a committee made up of representatives of the education administration, teachers from the setting and members of the school council as well as a Centre Leader/School Head of a setting that provides the same type of education. In Spain this can be a separate first cycle nursery unit for under 3 year-olds, a second cycle pre-primary unit in a primary school for 3 to under 6 year-olds or a combined, age-integrated centre. Applicants who pass the selection process are required to complete a management training programme (Ancheta-Arrabal 2024).

5.2.3 Job responsibilities

Across countries, systems and sectors, the responsibilities of Centre Leaders fall under four broad categories. These are related to: pedagogical and programme quality; staff support and staff management; partnerships and collaboration; strategic management and administration. Here we present a selection of the reported responsibilities.

5.2.3.1 Pedagogical and programme quality

- Guiding and supervising the pedagogical activities in accordance with national/federal state curricular goals and quality frameworks
- Developing a centre-specific educational programme with the team
- Leading the work in planning, documentation and evaluation
- Observing, monitoring and analysing pedagogical activities
- Allocating resources according to the children's needs and the conditions of the setting
- Designing the environment with access to both digital and other learning resources
- Ensuring the didactic approaches and work methods benefit children's participation
- Ensuring that children with special educational needs receive the support and challenges they need with participation of the parents/guardians
- Taking active measures against discrimination and abusive treatment
- Ensuring the health, safety and protection of children
- Ensuring the rights of children and the rights and duties of adults.

5.2.3.2 Staff support and staff management

- Creating an inspiring working environment
- Ensuring appropriate working conditions for all staff (pedagogical, support, housekeeping, cleaning)

- Supervising team development and coordination
- Supporting staff reflection and self-management
- Coordinating the mentoring, work shadowing and support of students on field practice
- Guiding, assisting and supervising younger teachers in their work
- Holding staff appraisal talks
- Providing and/or facilitating professional development opportunities on a regular basis and motivating all staff to participate
- Recruiting new professionals, preparing job descriptions
- Proposing the promotion of staff to job titles and pay grades
- Controlling teachers' compliance with the relevant legislation and regulations
- Recruiting specialist support staff
- Supervising on-site specialist support staff and coordinating with regional counselling centres.

5.2.3.3   Partnerships and collaboration

- Initiating and leading partnerships between educational institutions and relevant services and organisations
- Cooperating with the service provider and all other partners in the neighbourhood and region
- Organising diverse forms of cooperation with parents and informing them of changes in the rights and obligations of children, trainees and students
- Representing the ECEC centre before the responsible authorities in all pedagogical matters
- Developing (in *Sweden*) supportive forms of cooperation with the preschool class, the school and school-age *educare* provision
- Encouraging the participation of parents/guardians, local and municipal representatives in the planning and evaluation of educational activities
- In *Italy*, promoting and supporting relationships between 0–3 educational services, pre-primary schools and the municipal administration to support the goal of a unitary system
- Contributing to planning policies for young children and families at the local level.

5.2.3.4   Strategic management and administration

- Planning, managing, monitoring and developing the entire activities of the ECEC centre (organisation, coordination, supervision/control; education and upbringing; health and safety; social and humanitarian issues; financial matters)
- Supervising and monitoring the centre's objectives and programme in compliance with requirements of state bodies at the national and local level

- Managing the internal organisation of the ECEC centre and deciding on the expedient use of financial resources
- Organising and steering systematic quality assurance, improvement and development measures based on internal self-evaluation, and with the participation of parents
- Preparing annually a pedagogical supervision plan, a work plan, a kindergarten development plan and a self-evaluation report
- Submitting a written report to the local authority and the Board of Trustees once a year – on curricular and financial issues and any regulations required by a supervisory agency
- Compiling statistical data and transmitting them to the school inspectorate
- Conducting the administrative work of the setting (correspondence, implementation of circulars, operating regulations…)
- Contracting works, services and supplies of materials and technical equipment for the administrative and pedagogical activities
- Organising admission procedures.

Ukraine is one of the few countries to have issued *professional standards* specifically for the job profile of ECEC Directors. They focus on five dimensions of centre leadership (see Box 2).

Box 2

Professional standards for ECEC directors in Ukraine (2021)	
Organising a healthy, safe and inclusive learning environment	– Health protection – Planning and analysing the effectiveness of the educational process
Managing an EC centre	– Operational management (ability to secure the financing of the kindergarten, organisation and control of nutrition and medical services in the kindergarten, management of human resources) – Organisational-methodological (ability to organise the educational programme, the work of the psychological-pedagogical support team, the methodological support of the pedagogical staff) – Communication (ability to communicate effectively with all participants involved in the educational process and other stakeholders).
Ongoing personal and professional development	– Life-long learning (ability to reflect and self-assess, to plan professional development) – Ability to use ICT and e-resources effectively in the educational process, to be aware of and use safety rules in the digital environment.
Leadership and partnership	– Leadership (ability to present the early childhood institution/kindergarten, to show resilience and flexibility, to

	support conflict resolution and the prevention of professional burn-out) − Emotional-ethical (ability relating to self-regulation, to display tolerance, to conduct constructive and sustainable interactions with the participants of the educational process).
Strategic development	− Strategic governance and strategic development (ability to conduct strategic planning, to develop a strategy for the kindergarten, to develop a system of quality control) − Strategic communication (ability to present the kindergarten to different stakeholders) − Normative-legal (ability to use legal documents in the professional activities).

Source: Ukrainian Ministry of Economics 2021, in: Sofii 2024

5.3 Assistant co-workers

Assistant co-workers are defined here as people who support the core professional in the day-to-day running of the ECEC centre, but who in most countries are not independently responsible for educational tasks. A basic distinction can be made between assistants with and without relevant vocational training. As a rule, those with a formal certificate have a lower level qualification than the core practitioners (usually a secondary vocational education at ISCED level 3).

In the group of countries with a *unitary* ECEC system (Table 14), assistants are employed in each of the ten countries, albeit with different formal requirements. In *Finland, Sweden* and *Slovenia*, an ISCED 3 qualification is needed, in *Estonia* and *Lithuania* an ISCED 4 certification. Vocational training programmes can last between around six months (*Lithuania*) and four years (*Slovenia*) and may have varying specialisations. In *Finland*, for example, a 'Childcare Worker' follows a social and health care track, whereas in *Sweden* they specialise in pedagogical work. It is striking that in four countries – *Denmark, Latvia, Norway* and *Ukraine* – assistants can be employed without formal qualifications. However, there are recommendations that they should have such qualifications and/or complete a relevant course (e.g. on first aid). In *Denmark*, an increasing number of assistants now have an ISCED 3 qualification (although only 6% to date). In *Croatia*, assistants do not work on a regular basis and mostly support children with special needs.

Table 14
Assistant co-workers – formal qualification requirements in unitary ECEC systems

	Qualification required?
Croatia	Further education course with a focus on children with developmental delays
Denmark	No
Estonia	ISCED 4
Finland	ISCED 3
Latvia	No
Lithuania	ISCED 4
Norway	No
Slovenia	ISCED 3
Sweden	ISCED 3
Ukraine	No

Sources: SEEPRO-3 workforce reports, in: Oberhuemer/Schreyer 2024b

In most countries with a *part-integrated* ECEC system (Table 15), assistants have a qualification at ISCED 3 level or higher. Exceptions to this are *Romania*, where only 30 hours of further training are required every five years to work as an assistant in pre-primary education (3–5 years), and the private, voluntary and independent sectors of the four nations of the *United Kingdom*, where no relevant qualification is required. In *Italy* and *Malta*, there are no assistants in pre-primary and kindergarten settings for over 3 year-olds. In *Spain*, the 2006 Education Act stipulates that only qualified staff may work in educational institutions with children aged 0–6, but sometimes assistants are employed who are responsible for non-educational work and have a lower qualification (ISCED 3) than the core practitioners.

Table 15
Assistant co-workers – formal qualification requirements in part-integrated ECEC systems

	Assistants in ECEC settings for under 3 or under 4 year-olds	Assistants in ECEC settings for children over 3 or over 4 years of age up to primary school entry
Austria	ISCED 3 (since 2019)	
Germany	ISCED 3	
Italy	Varies across municipalities	No assistant co-workers
Luxembourg	ISCED 3	ISCED 4
Malta	ISCED 3 (since 2023)	No assistant co-workers
Romania	ISCED 4	30 hours CPD every 5 years
Russia	ISCED 3 or 4	
Serbia	ISCED 4	
Spain	ISCED 3*	
United Kingdom	No relevant qualification required in the PVI sectors	

*The Education Act 2006 stipulates that all staff in ECEC centres must be qualified. Specific requirements vary among the Autonomous Communities.
Sources: SEEPRO-3 workforce reports 2024, in: Oberhuemer/Schreyer 2024b

In six of the 13 countries with a *bi-sectoral* ECEC system (Table 16), no assistants work in the childcare sectors. In *Ireland* and the *Czech Republic*, no qualification is required to work as an assistant; in *Hungary*, a 20-hour course must be completed. Only in *Cyprus, France, Greece* and *Portugal* is a qualification at ISCED level 3 or 4 required.

The situation for assistants in the respective education sectors looks quite different. *Belgium* and Sl*ovakia* have the highest formal requirement at ISCED level 4; in *The Netherlands* either ISCED 4 or 3 is required; in *Bulgaria, Cyprus*, the *Czech Republic, France* and *Portugal*, assistants have a qualification at ISCED 3 level. No formal qualification is required in *Hungary, Ireland, Poland* or *Switzerland*. *Greece* is the only country in which no assistants are employed in the education sector (pre-primary schools for 4 and 5 year-olds).

Table 16
Assistant co-workers – formal qualification requirements in bi-sectoral systems

	Assistants in the childcare sectors	Assistants in the education sectors
Belgium	None	ISCED 4
Bulgaria	None	ISCED 3
Cyprus	ISCED 3	ISCED 3
Czech Republic	No relevant qualification required	ISCED 3 (since 2016)
France	ISCED 3	ISCED 3
Greece	ISCED 3 oder 4	None
Hungary	No relevant qualification required, but 20-hour course mandatory	No relevant qualification required, 400-hour course an option
Ireland	No relevant qualification required	No relevant qualification required
The Netherlands	None	ISCED 3 or 4
Poland	None	No relevant qualification required
Portugal	ISCED 3	ISCED 3
Slovakia	None	ISCED 4
Switzerland	None	No relevant qualification required

Sources: SEEPRO-3 workforce reports 2024, in: Oberhuemer/Schreyer 2024b

A look at the different ECEC systems shows that assistants are more frequently employed in the *part-integrated* countries than in the *bi-sectoral* systems, and that they generally have a qualification at ISCED level 3 or 4. Assistants in the childcare sectors of the latter tend to be rare and only in four countries (*Cyprus, France, Greece* and *Portugal*) do they have a qualification.

Moreover, if we take into account the proportion of low-skilled or unqualified staff in the SEEPRO-3 countries (see chapter 5.6), we see that in some countries that employ assistants with recognised qualifications, unqualified staff also work in ECEC. In *Sweden*, for example, 28% of staff in municipal ECEC centres and 41% in private ECEC centres are unqualified or only slightly qualified, in *Denmark* the figure is more than a third and in *Austria* more than 40% of all staff.

5.4 ECEC counsellors, supervisors and inspectors

In most SEEPRO-3 countries, ECEC centres are supported by specialist counselling staff in various ways. ECEC counsellors can have an advisory function as well as a monitoring or inspection function – and sometimes both. ECEC counsellors cover a wide range of activities, including quality assurance and quality development, management and team counselling, supporting the implementation of pedagogical-curricular guidelines or providing advice on legal issues. As specialist supervisors or inspectors, they are also responsible for reviewing the quality of the work carried out by the staff and leaders of ECEC centres or for external evaluations. Specialist *counsellors* are usually employed by the service provider, working in or with a number of centres as required; in a few cases they may also be recruited from the ECEC centre staff. Specialist *supervisors* or *inspectors* are employed externally.

5.4.1 Tasks between counselling, supervision and inspection

In three of the ten countries with *unitary* ECEC systems – *Croatia*, *Lithuania* and *Norway* – there are no legal provisions for specialist staff who have a counselling, coaching or professional support function. Inspections are carried out by external bodies – in *Croatia*, for example, this is the Agency for Education and Teacher Training, a subordinate authority of the Ministry of Education. In the remaining seven countries with a unitary system, the focus is mostly on advising the ECEC centre teams and leaders. One example is *Sweden*, where the staff with an advisory, coaching and support function focus on the work team in order to further develop the competence of the professionals and the overall quality of the ECEC centre. In *Denmark* and *Ukraine*, ECEC counsellors have both advisory and supervisory functions.

In *Estonia*, support *within* the ECEC centres is not provided by one person, but by a board of trustees. Every ECEC centre has this kind of committee, which comprises representatives of the centre staff, the parents, the provider and/or the local authority. The focus here is more on the supervisory function, e.g. with regard to drawing up a budget or the appropriate use of funds. However, the board also has the task of ensuring that the educational programme in the ECEC centre corresponds to the developmental needs and interests of the children.

In three of the seven countries with advisory staff, these work directly in the ECEC centre. In *Latvia*, for example, a coordinator (*methodologista*) or an 'expert in learning guidance' works in every centre; in *Ukraine*, an early education methodology specialist supports staff directly in the ECEC centre; and in *Slovenia*, in most public ECEC centres an in-house advisory service has the task of working together with the staff and centre leaders, focussing in particular on the optimal development of children with special needs. In *Denmark, Finland* and *Sweden,* ECEC counsellors are employed by the municipalities and work across a number of facilities. In *Sweden*, these 'Pedagogical Leaders' (also known as development or process managers) focus on the competence requirements, areas of responsibility and distribution of tasks within the ECEC centres and are responsible, for example, for quality assurance and addressing the CPD needs and wishes of the centre staff.

In the *part-integrated* ECEC systems, only in *Luxembourg* and *Malta* are there no legal provisions for specialist counsellors in the ECEC field. In the remaining eight countries, counselling and advisory staff work across several ECEC centres. They are employed by youth welfare offices and/or service providers (*Germany*), are appointed by the local authority (*Romania*) or are employed by education inspectorates (*Spain*). Only the country reports from *Russia* and *Serbia* emphasise inspection as the task of these specialists, who are employed by state or municipal education authorities. Otherwise, in the other six countries, tasks include both counselling activities and supervisory functions. In *Austria*, one of the tasks of specialist counsellors is to accompany young professionals; however, depending on the federal state, the supervisory function tends to be more in focus than the counselling function. In *Spain*, ECEC inspectors monitor educational institutions from a pedagogical and organisational perspective, prepare reports and coordinate academic and vocational guidance activities.

In *Germany,* ECEC counsellors (*Fachberaterinnen/Fachberater*), who are mostly employed by the service providers, have a supporting, coordinating and in some cases controlling role. From the perspective of field experts, the importance of their support function for Centre Leaders in their tasks of quality, personnel and organisational development, as well as their role in the transfer of knowledge between research and professional practice, is undisputed. Nevertheless, ECEC counselling is currently organised in very diverse ways in terms of mandate and responsibility, both in the 16 federal states and among the providers of early childhood education and care settings. Furthermore, specified job descriptions rarely exist and the legal framework conditions in the federal states vary considerably (Kaiser/Fuchs-Rechlin 2020; Oberhuemer/Schreyer 2024a).

The Pedagogical Coordinators in *Italy* (*coordinatori pedagogici*) currently play a strategic role in the implementation of the emerging integrated 0–6 ECEC system by promoting pedagogical continuity between nurseries and pre-primary schools and supporting pedagogical professionals in reflecting on their practice. In addition, networks of Pedagogical Coordinators at the regional or district level are responsible for research and innovation in the early childhood sector and thus for constantly reflecting on the principles underlying the entire educational programme. In more recent legislation (2017), the role of *coordinatori pedagogici* has been redefined and expanded. Their remit now covers the entire education system, not just early childhood education (Picchio/Bove 2024).

According to the SEEPRO-3 country reports regarding the *bi-sectoral* systems, there are differences between the childcare and education sectors in terms of ECEC counselling concepts. For example, there are no specialist counselling posts in the childcare sectors of *Bulgaria,* the *Czech Republic, Greece* and *Slovakia* and, and they are very rare in the *French Community of Belgium*. Since 2021, however, new posts for Pedagogical Coaches have been created in the *Flemish Community of Belgium* with a counselling function in crèche facilities.

The counselling function is also a priority in the education sectors of the *French Community of Belgium, Bulgaria* and *France*. In contrast, the inspection function is predominant in the childcare sectors in *France* and *Ireland* as well as in the education sectors in *Cyprus, The Netherlands, Poland, Portugal* and *Switzerland.*

ECEC counsellors with both advisory and supervisory functions can be found in the childcare sectors of the *French* and *German-speaking communities of Belgium, The Netherlands* and *Hungary*, as well as in the education sectors of the *Czech Republic, Greece* (kindergartens for 4- and 5 year-olds) and *Slovakia*. Tasks are varied: in the *French* childcare sector, specialist advisers support staff in implementing the education plan, but they also have a supervisory function in evaluating the staff and checking the functioning of the crèches; in the education sector in *France*, they accompany trainee teachers and organise pedagogical support on site. In *Portugal*, Pedagogical Coordinators for pre-primary education are part of the organisation of each school cluster in the public sector and their tasks are to monitor pedagogical activities, promote cooperation and assess teaching staff.

Specialist counselling in *Slovakia* takes place via institution-specific advisory boards: a pedagogical advisory board, a methods advisory board and a kindergarten advisory board. The first two are internal support committees within the setting with a focus on pedagogical and didactic issues. The kindergarten advisory board, which is made up of representatives from the ECEC centre, parents and kindergarten staff, contributes to quality improvement, proposes innovations – and also reviews the procedures and activities of the kindergarten.

Most country reports indicate that ECEC advisory and supervisory staff are employed externally and work across services. This is the case in *Poland,* where settings for under 3 year-olds are administratively supervised by the municipalities, while for the kindergartens for over 3 year-olds so-called 'territorial units' are responsible for coordination and supervision. In the *Czech Republic*, school counselling centres carry out assessments and offer advice to kindergartens; if necessary, staff can attend a relevant CPD programme via the National Pedagogical Institute.

In *The Netherlands*, childcare service providers have been obliged since 2019 to provide the managers of childcare settings with Pedagogical Coaches or Management Assistants who support both the pedagogical work as well as assessments and analyses.

5.4.2 Qualification requirements for ECEC advisory and supervisory posts

Generally speaking, ECEC specialists with counselling, supervisory or coordinating tasks are usually qualified core professionals with an ISCED 6 level qualification who may have completed additional further training. This is the case for the seven countries with a *unitary* ECEC system which employ counselling staff.

The minimum qualification required is more variable in the *part-integrated* ECEC systems: while in *Italy*, for example, a Master's degree is the rule for the post of Pedagogical Coordinator, as is also the case for Educational Advisers in *Romania*, there are no uniform qualification requirements in *Austria* or *Germany*; however, in *Austria* ECEC counsellors generally hold a full qualification as an Early Childhood Pedagogue (ISCED 5 or 6), several years of relevant professional experience and relevant additional training.

The *bi-sectoral* ECEC systems present a particularly varied picture when it comes to qualification requirements for counselling and advisory posts. There are no regulated qualification requirements for the childcare sector in *France* or for the education sector in *The Netherlands*, where regular teachers are usually granted a certain number of hours for coordinating tasks. In other countries, a Bachelor's degree or equivalent qualification is usually required, as in the *Flemish Community of Belgium*, the childcare sector of the *French Community of Belgium* and in *Poland*. The same applies to the education sectors in *Greece* (where 15 years of professional experience are also needed) and *Slovakia*. The specialist staff with advisory tasks in the childcare sector in *Cyprus* generally have a Bachelor's degree, whereas coordinating staff in the education sector usually have a Master's degree. The latter is also the qualification requirement for inspectors in the education sector in *France* (with an additional examination) and *Poland*. In *Bulgaria*, specialist advisory functions are performed by Senior Pre-primary Teachers (with an ISCED 6 level qualification, ten years of professional experience and additional further training) and Head

Pre-primary Teachers (who hold a Master's degree, plus further training and 'outstanding' assessments).

In summary, it can be concluded that there is no such thing as 'the' ECEC counsellor or supervisor in the SEEPRO-3 countries. Even though there are often special posts for counselling, supervision, coaching and other supporting structures for ECEC centre staff, the professional profiles of these specialists often differ depending on the kind of ECEC system, whether they are located in the childcare or education sector and whether or not there are specific qualification requirements for holding such a post.

5.5 Specialist support staff

Staff with a field of specialisation beyond the regular qualification of the core practitioner are deployed in different ways in ECEC centres across the 33 SEEPRO-3 countries, mainly to support children, but also staff and parents. In some cases, they are specially qualified professionals within the centre, but more often ECEC centres are supported by specialists from external agencies. These may be Psychologists, Speech Therapists, Physiotherapists, Curative and Remedial Education specialists, subject specialists such as Music or Sport teachers, or specialists with methodological skills. In *Ukraine*, for example, ECEC centres can employ an Early Childhood Teacher Methodologist, a Special Needs Pedagogue, a Speech Therapist, an Educational Psychologist, a Music Teacher, a Sports Instructor, and a Handicraft Teacher for a specified number of hours per week. It is the Centre Head's responsibility to develop and approve the job descriptions for each post according to the Ukrainian National Classification of Professions (Sofii 2024).

Overall, the tasks of these support specialists are similar: besides providing expertise in subjects such as drama or sport, they usually focus on children with special educational needs; they observe individual children and create support measures; they try to create a suitable educational environment for the children; they may work with individual children or groups of children; they advise professionals and parents; they cooperate with relevant services; they promote inclusion processes; depending on their training, they also make diagnoses and carry out tests, examinations or therapies.

Across all SEEPRO-3 countries, support provided by in-house professionals is on the whole less frequent.

However, in countries with *unitary* ECEC systems, this kind of specialist support staff is significantly more common than in the other ECEC system types, namely in eight of the ten countries: *Estonia, Finland, Croatia, Latvia, Lithuania, Norway, Slovenia and Ukraine*. Some examples:

In *Croatia*, kindergartens with more than 200 children can employ Special Needs Pedagogues, Psychologists and rehabilitation experts such as Speech and Language Therapists, Social Pedagogues or Curative Educators (Bouillet 2024). In *Estonia*, a Healthcare professional works in the ECEC centre on a daily basis: these medical experts monitor the children's health, ensure that state health and safety regulations are adhered to, inform parents and the child's doctor of any health problems and advise parents and teachers on health issues (Veisson/Peterson 2024). Support professionals in *Lithuania* include Psychologists, Socio-educational assistants, Public Health Counsellors and Language Trainers; most of them work regularly in the institution and have a designated working space there (Sabaliauskas/Siarova 2024). In public kindergartens in *Slovenia*, on-site advisory services that work with the staff and management in planning, monitoring and evaluating the kindergarten programme for children with special needs. The specialists include Psychologists, Pedagogues, Social Workers, Social Pedagogues and Special Needs support staff (Jager 2024).

In *Denmark* and *Sweden*, it is more common to make use of external specialist services. For example, Danish ECEC centres may be supported by specialist support staff assigned to them by the local authority's educational-psychological advisory service. In *Sweden*, ECEC centres have access to so-called resource teams which accompany and support the core practitioners in their daily work. As a rule, they do not work directly with the children, but refer them to appropriate specialist services if necessary, which carry out individual counselling sessions with the parents/guardians and the children (Karlsson Lohmander 2024).

In-house support staff tend to be rare in countries with a *part-integrated* ECEC system. Two exceptions are *Serbia* and *Luxembourg*. In *Serbia*, the law stipulates that every ECEC must employ an 'Expert Associate', either a Pedagogist or a Psychologist. Centres with 24 to 48 groups can employ an additional support specialist and centres with more than 48 groups can also employ a Speech Therapist or a specialist for Art, Music and Sport (Miskeljin 2024). In *Luxembourg*, each ECEC centre appoints a Pedagogical Coordinator for Multilingual Education and a specialist for Inclusive Education, whose task it is to deal with pedagogical issues in their area of expertise and to design and coordinate the implementation of multilingual or inclusive education (de Moll et al. 2024).

Otherwise, most countries with *part-integrated* ECEC systems make use of external specialist services that are deployed as required (e.g. *Austria, Germany, Malta, Romania, Spain*). In *Malta*, for example, Inclusion Coordinators are responsible for all issues relating to inclusion in childcare centres for under 3 year-olds. In kindergartens for 3 and 4 year-olds, Early Intervention specialists are responsible for supporting the implementation of the educational programme with regard to inclusion; in some cases, there are also specialist staff for Music, Drama or Sport (Sollars 2024). In *Spain*, pedagogical and psycho-educational counselling teams for early childhood education provide support for social integration or healthcare, among other things (Ancheta-Arrabal 2024). In the *UK*, the protection of children or specific tasks in special education are the responsibility of professionals from the ECEC centre, but there is also additional external support from Health Advisers, Social Workers or Speech Therapists (Lumsden 2024).

External support professionals also predominate in countries with *a bi-sectoral* ECEC system, such as in the *Flemish* and *German-speaking Communities of Belgium, Ireland, Portugal, Switzerland,* and in the education sectors of *Cyprus* and the *Czech Republic*. In *Cyprus*, public ECEC centres are visited by Educational Psychologists, Remedial Teachers, Speech or Occupational Therapists at certain times; among other things, they carry out diagnoses of children with special needs or work with children with communication disorders (Loizou 2024). The childcare sector in the *Czech Republic* does not provide for support professionals. In *Portugal*, the national system for early childhood intervention with teams of Early Childhood Teachers, Nurses, Psychologists and other therapists is responsible for identifying children for intervention measures; services organised by the Ministry of Education support professionals in defining strategies (Araújo 2024).

5.6 Staff in ECEC settings by qualification and gender: an overview

In all ten SEEPRO-3 countries with a *unitary* ECEC system, a Bachelor's degree (ISCED 6) is the minimum qualification requirement for core professionals working with children from a very early age until they start school. At least three quarters of professionals in *Estonia, Lithuania* and *Ukraine* are qualified to this level. Staff with a previously accepted qualification at a lower level or a non-specialist qualification make up the remainder of core professionals in these three countries. In comparison, the proportion of university-educated professionals is lower in the Nordic countries and in *Slovenia*, where in *Denmark, Norway* and *Sweden* those with a Bachelor degree or higher make up just over half of all professionals and only 39% in *Finland*. Moreover, the proportion of staff with another, non-relevant qualification or no qualification at all is quite high. In *Denmark*, for example, this is 36.9% of the workforce, in *Norway* 25.8%.

The proportion of males in the workforce is mostly low and ranges from less than 1% (*Estonia* and *Lithuania*) to 4.4% (*Croatia*). Only in *Norway* (10.7%), *Denmark* (9.5%) and in the pre-school classes in *Sweden* (8.4%) is the proportion of men working as pedagogical specialists comparatively high.

In three of the ten SEEPRO-3 countries[10] with a *part-integrated* ECEC system (*Malta, Austria, Russia*), core professionals are not required to have a Bachelor's degree. In *Malta*, the proportion of qualified staff with a Bachelor's degree is higher in kindergarten centres for 3 and 4 year-olds than in childcare centres for under 3 year-olds. In the kindergartens, 13% of the specialised staff in state kindergartens, 16% in church kindergartens and 12% in private kindergartens have a Bachelor's degree. However, the majority of pedagogical staff have a qualification at ISCED/EQF 4 level. In the childcare centres, only 2% of staff have a Bachelor's degree. Here too, the majority of staff (55%) has a qualification at ISCED 4 level; moreover, around 22% have no specialist qualification at all. Just under half of the workforce in *Austria* has completed a vocational qualification classified at ISCED level 5, whereas a high proportion of staff (42%) have either a low-level qualification or no qualification at all. In *Russia*, although more than half of regular Kindergarten Teachers have a higher education qualification, the remainder have the minimum requirement of a post-secondary qualification.

In the pre-school classes of the formal education sector in *Luxembourg* for 4 and 5 year-olds, almost three quarters (72.8%) of professionals have a university degree, whereas in the non-formal sector the proportion is slightly less than a quarter.[11] In *Germany*, two thirds of the workforce has a post-secondary qualification and only just under 6% a Bachelor's degree. However, since the post-secondary vocational award is also classified at ISCED level 6, i.e. as equivalent to a Bachelor's degree, the overall picture is one of a highly qualified workforce.

As in countries with a unitary ECEC system, the proportion of male professionals is relatively low,[12] ranging from less than 1% in *Malta* and *Italy* to 7% in *Luxembourg* and almost 8% in *Germany*.

Generally speaking, in the 13 countries with a *bi-sectoral* ECEC system the proportion of university-educated professionals in pre-school educational settings for children aged 3 years and above (in some cases 2 and above) is significantly higher than in settings for under 3 year-olds. Nearly all core professionals in the education sectors have a higher education qualification, with only the *Czech Republic* (ca. 22%) and *Slovakia* (ca. 9%) lagging behind because of the lower minimum requirements. Otherwise, the proportion of professionals with a higher education degree ranges from 3% in the childcare sector in

---

10 No relevant data for *Italy, Serbia, Spain, UK-Wales, Scotland* and *Northern Ireland.*
11 However, the data for the non-formal sector is not representative and from 2016.
12 No recent data for *Russia, Romania, UK-Wales* and *UK-Northern Ireland.*

the *French Community of Belgium* to 34.4% in the non-primary sector in *Ireland*.

The proportion of male staff in the bi-sectoral ECEC systems also tends to be higher in the education sectors than in the childcare sectors.

6 Initial professional education of core practitioners

A note on terminology
We have chosen the term 'initial professional education' (IPE) to describe the academic-vocational preparation of those wishing to work in the early childhood field. We prefer this to the concept of 'training,' which tends to have narrower, more mechanistic and utilitarian connotations and does not explicitly include the wider goals, values and philosophies which are the foundations of a professional approach to educating and caring for young children. Education, if seen in its broader sense (Fielding/Moss 2011), represents this more comprehensive understanding and emphasises that the pathway towards becoming an ECEC professional is about the unfolding personal journey of the educator as well as about acquiring the knowledge, competences and skills needed for working individually and collectively with young children up to primary school entry age.

6.1 What competences do ECEC core practitioners need? Competence profiles in six countries

One of the first European studies to look specifically at competence requirements for early childhood education and care was the CoRe study (Urban/Vandenbroeck et al. 2011). CoRe moved beyond a narrowly defined person-related understanding of 'competence' and highlighted the need for a systemic understanding in order to build a professional system of early childhood education and care. The 'competent system' develops in reciprocal relationships between individuals, teams, institutions and the wider socio-political context "… and a key feature… is its support for individuals to realise their capability to develop responsible and responsive practices that respond to the needs of children and families in ever-changing societal contexts (Urban/Vandenbroeck et al. 2011: 21)."

The competence requirements presented in the SEEPRO-3 study are predominantly person-oriented and occupation-related, since they represent goals to be strived for or achieved during the initial professional education (IPE) of prospective early childhood professionals. However, it is important to remember that becoming 'competent' for this complex field of activity is an ongoing process that not only requires a sound foundation of professional knowledge and field-relevant skills but also involves developing professional values and the reflective competences needed to work in highly complex, unpredictable and diverse contexts.

Based on this understanding, what is presented in this chapter focuses specifically on competence requirements for core practitioners, i.e. group-leading pedagogues. In many of the SEEPRO-3 country reports, competence specifications for co-workers or for special needs professionals are also included; however, constraints of space prevent us from analysing them here. For the same reason, we are unable to present a comprehensive overview of the sometimes very detailed 'competence catalogues'. We have therefore decided to select two examples from each of the three ECEC system types in order to pinpoint some of the similarities and differences in country-specific competence requirements.

In general, there are three main types of competence specifications for early childhood pedagogy professionals:

- Competence frameworks for ECEC based on national legislation (as in *Hungary, Italy*); in some countries these frameworks are called Professional Standards (e.g. in *Croatia, Estonia, Russia, Serbia*).
- Competence requirements defined by individual IPE institutions, particularly universities (as in, e.g., *Finland, Greece, Malta, Slovenia, Sweden*).
- Standards in highly privatised childcare systems (as in *The Netherlands*) may be defined by childcare provider organisations in the sense of industrial standards.

For closer analysis we have selected six countries: *Germany, Hungary, Italy, The Netherlands, Norway, Slovenia*. We have chosen these countries because among them they represent:

- Different ECEC system types
- Central/eastern and western European states
- State-level and university-level competence definitions
- Different core practitioner profiles
- Varying formal levels of initial professional education.

6.1.1 Competence profiles[13] in two unitary ECEC systems: Norway and Slovenia

Whereas in *Norway*, competence specifications are embedded in a national curricular framework plan for Kindergarten Teacher Education (2013), in *Slovenia* they are defined by the three universities offering Bachelor study programmes for prospective ECEC professionals. Both countries have the same

---

13 All the competence profiles presented below have been significantly shortened by the authors of this publication. The detailed versions can be found in the respective SEEPRO-3 ECEC workforce profile reports: https://www.seepro.eu.

core practitioner profile and the same formal qualification requirement: an Early Childhood Pedagogy Professional with an ISCED 6 level qualification.

In *Norway*, the national framework plan specifies learning outcomes regarding knowledge, skills and general competence. It encompasses four broad knowledge areas (see Table 17). In the final year of studies, the main focus is on management, cooperation and development work as well as in-depth specialisation; it is concluded with a Bachelor thesis. This kind of competence specification is essentially a curricular orientation framework for the IPE of ECEC professionals.

Table 17
Norway: Competence areas in the IPE route for Early Childhood Pedagogy Professionals

Knowledge area	ECTS credits	Year of study
1. Children's development, play and learning	20	Years 1 and 2
2. Society, religion, philosophy of life and ethics	20	Years 1 and 2
3. Language, texts and mathematics	20	Years 1 and 2
4. Nature, health and movement	20	Years 1 and 2
Specialisation in two of the areas above	40	Year 3
Management, cooperation and development work	15	Year 3
In-depth specialisation	30	Year 3
Bachelor thesis	15	Year 3
Total	**180**	

Source: Norwegian Ministry of Education and Research 2012, in: Gulbrandsen 2024

In *Slovenia*, three universities (Ljubljana, Maribor, Primorska) provide Bachelor-level study programmes for prospective ECEC core professionals. Each has its own competence specifications. Required competences as defined by the University of Ljubljana Faculty of Education (2023; Jager 2024) are, for example:

– *General competence requirements:* knowledge and understanding of the social systems (in particular the education system); knowledge of educational concepts, their philosophical and historical foundations; knowledge of and compliance with the institutional frameworks of work (requirements, legislation, documentation requirements, legal aspects of educational work); understanding individual values and value systems, management of professional-ethical issues; knowledge, understanding, focusing on inclusive, non-discriminatory work, multiculturalism.

– *Occupation-specific competences:* understanding and applying curricular theories as well as general and didactic knowledge of the subject; recognising and evaluating children's abilities and achievements and giving feedback; knowing and understanding theoretical principles of counselling; knowledge of working forms, contents and methods as well as independent implementation of the kindergarten curriculum and the curriculum for Year 1 primary school; ensuring children's emotional security and promoting their autonomy according to their maturity.

Among the other eight countries with *unitary* ECEC systems, the report from *Croatia* emphasises that the occupational standard for ECEC Teachers was entered into the register of the Croatian Qualifications Framework in 2023. This means that the qualification standards have yet to be adopted and implemented in the IPE study programmes and that competence and curricular specifications continue to be defined at the level of the higher education institution – and these still vary considerably (Bouillet 2024).

6.1.2 Competence profiles in two part-integrated ECEC systems: Germany and Italy

In both *Germany* and *Italy*, competence frameworks for the early childhood profession(s) have been defined at the supra-regional level. In *Germany*, as a federal country, the framework is based on a resolution adopted in 2011 by the Standing Conference of the Education Ministers of the 16 federal states and amended in 2017 (KMK 2017). In *Italy*, the competence specifications are defined by national legislation and there are two sets, one for the professionals working in ECEC services for under 3 year-olds and one for those working in pre-primary settings for children aged 3 up to school entry. The professional profiles in both countries differ. In *Germany*, the core practitioners working with children across the ECEC phase are Social and Childhood Pedagogy Professionals, as are the Educators working with under 3 year-olds in *Italy*, since in both cases they can also work in other social-pedagogical fields. The core practitioners in the *scuole dell'infanzia* are school teachers with a Pre-primary and Primary Education Professional profile.

In *Germany*, the Competence-Oriented Qualification Profile issued by the KMK (2017) defines six fields of learning and the relevant areas of knowledge and competence. The Qualification Profile is very detailed and only a selection of the competences and skills that prospective Educators are expected to possess at the end of their mostly three-year course of initial professional education studies is presented here. Each federal state implements the Qualification Profile in its own legislation. The orientation for this is a cross-state curriculum (KMK 2020), and the competences described in the curriculum are mandatory for the vocational technical colleges of social pedagogy, where the main core practitioners in ECEC settings (Educators – *Erzieher/Erzieherinnen*) are qualified (KMK 2011/2017, 15-28; adapted, Oberhuemer/Schreyer 2024a):

- *Learning area 1*: understanding children, adolescents and young adults in their living environment and shaping pedagogical relationships with them (e.g. independently aligning, planning and designing pedagogical concepts to the living environments of children, adolescents and young adults)
- *Learning area 2:* stimulating, supporting and guiding developmental and educational processes (e.g. reflecting on and further developing own educational experiences and competences in the various educational and learning areas)
- *Learning area 3:* guiding pedagogical work in groups (e.g. conceptually anchoring participation structures for children, adolescents and young adults
- *Learning area 4:* building educational partnerships with parents and caregivers (e.g. identifying the different individual needs and resources of families and caregivers, assessing them in a systematic way and reviewing framework conditions and services on this basis)
- *Learning area 5:* developing the institution and team (e.g. participating in needs and inventory analyses for the socio-pedagogical institution in order to incorporate these into conceptual planning)
- *Learning area 6:* cooperating in networks and organising transitions (e.g. organising transitions systematically on the basis of research evidence and conceptual frameworks).

In the context of the emerging integrated 0–6 system in *Italy*, a Bachelor's degree has only recently become a mandatory minimum qualification for Educators working in centres for children under the age of 3. The following five areas of competence define a specialisation in early education (at least 55 ECTS credits) as part of a broad three-year Bachelor's degree in education for prospective socio-pedagogical educators (Picchio/Bove 2024):

- *Cultural and psycho-educational competences*: e.g. knowledge of the pedagogical, sociological, psychological, anthropological, historical, philosophical and institutional aspects of the early education of children aged 0–3 years and the needs of their parents
- *Methodological competences*: e.g. programming, observation, documentation and evaluation of early education quality
- *Technical and professional competences*: e.g. designing the environment, timetable and play materials according to the children's developmental needs and abilities
- *Relationship skills*: e.g. listening, observing, documenting and evaluating the quality of early education
- *Reflective competences*.

The five-year university degree in Primary and Preschool Education *(insegnante di scuola dell'infanzia)* in *Italy* aims to prepare both pre-primary and primary education teachers with all-round professional competence who are capable of fostering children's motivation, creativity and identity development while constructing flexible and complex learning programmes for the different subject areas, with a strong emphasis on transversal learning objectives. Students also receive guidance in the contents and methods of teaching of the subjects listed in the National Curricular Guidelines for Pre-primary and Primary Schools. Graduates should have acquired the following competences at the end of this degree programme:

- *Cultural, pedagogical and psychological competences*: knowledge in the field of educational science, with a focus on psycho-pedagogic and methodological and didactic competences.
- *Multidisciplinary competences* related to pre-primary and primary education.
- *Competences related to children with learning disabilities* and their welcoming into the school environment, with a focus on personalised didactic approaches and intervention.
- *Informatics/technological competences.*

6.1.3 Competence profiles in two bi-sectoral ECEC systems: Hungary and The Netherlands

In both *Hungary* and *The Netherlands,* the ECEC systems are 'split'. Ministries with different jurisdictions are responsible for ECEC services for under 3 year-olds (Hungary, Ministry of Culture and Innovation) or under 4 year-olds (The Netherlands, Ministry of Social Affairs and Employment) and pre-primary education for older children up to compulsory primary schooling. *Hungary* is the only country in Europe where kindergartens for 3 to 6 year-olds currently come under the Ministry of the Interior rather than the Ministry of Education.

In *Hungary*, the most common types of core professional in the nurseries for under 3 year-olds are either an Early Childhood Caregiver and Educator (*Kisgyermekgondozó, -nevelő),* with a post-secondary vocational qualification classified at EQF level 5, or an Infant and Early Childhood Educator (*Csecsemő és kisgyermeknevelő*) with an ISCED level 6 Bachelor's degree. In *The Netherlands*, the Pedagogical Workers in the childcare sector (*Pedagogisch Medewerker, Leidster*) have an ISCED 3 or 4 level qualification. According to the SEEPRO professional profiles, all three are classified as Early Childhood Pedagogy Professionals. The teachers who work with 4 and 5 year-olds in *The Netherlands* have an ISCED 6 level qualification as Pre-primary and Primary Education Professionals (*Leerkracht*).

In *Hungary*, for the childcare sector, 36 competence areas are defined for the one or two-year post-secondary vocational programme for the Early Childhood Caregiver and Educators who work with under 3 year-olds. These include both skills and abilities related to sector-specific *basic education* as well as those related to *specialist work* within the child welfare and child protection sector. The 18 competence areas for the latter are: understanding and using relevant legislation and literature; understanding and supporting children's development; applying an individual pedagogical and psychological approach to children; identifying atypical development; understanding different socio-cultural family backgrounds and supporting families; communication and cooperation; setting goals and planning processes based on pedagogical and psychological knowledge.

The university courses which qualify Infant and Early Childhood Educators (*Csecsemő és kisgyermeknevelő*) define competence profiles in a similar way to university courses for prospective Pre-primary Pedagogues (who work with 3 to 6 year-olds). These are structured according to four broad categories; (1) knowledge, (2) ability, (3) attitude, (4) autonomy and responsibility. *Knowledge* is expected to cover, for example, the development, characteristics, care, education, and feeding of young children; the options and methods of forming good habits; the legal framework of working with young children; the effects of family upbringing and the importance of early attachment; electronic information systems. *Abilities* include applying a holistic view towards educating and caring for the children; forming good relationships with the children, their families and other professionals; handling information and documenting children's development; communication skills. *Attitudes* include a reflective and empathic approach. *Autonomy and responsibility* includes making decisions, demonstrating responsibility, cooperating with other professionals, observing ethics, making compromises, working in teams (Korintus 2024).

In the childcare sector in *The Netherlands*, the competence requirements for Pedagogical Workers as defined by Branch/Industry Standards are organised into ten clusters focused on (1) the work with children and parents), (2) their functioning as a professional in the specific context and (3) their own professional development (EVC-Branchestandaard 2021; Singer/Romijn 2024):

Cluster 1: Caring for the emotional and physical wellbeing of children (e.g. sensitive responsiveness)
Cluster 2: Ensuring children's safety (e.g. creating a safe environment for discovery, practice and adventure)
Cluster 3: Following and stimulating children's development and learning (e.g. providing a balance between new and familiar activities)
Cluster 4: Supporting and stimulating play and leisure activities (e.g. enriching children's experiences)

Cluster 5: Supporting and stimulating autonomy, participation, citizenship (e.g. motivating children to engage in social activities and build friendships)
Cluster 6: Influencing the behaviour of and interaction between children (e.g. providing structure and setting boundaries)
Cluster 7: Establishing a partnership with the parents (e.g. sharing information with parents)
Cluster 8: Collaborating with colleagues and other professionals in the child's environment (e.g. stimulating each other as colleagues)
Cluster 9: Improving the service quality (e.g. evaluating and justifying work and actions)
Cluster 10: Developing in the profession (e.g. monitoring one's own working conditions).

For the Pre-primary and Primary School Teachers working with 4 and 5 year-olds in schools, the competence specifications are laid down in national legislation (Education Professions Act 2013). Seven competence requirements with Dublin Descriptors (knowing, applying, evaluating, communicating, learning to learn) are set out in the national curriculum of the teacher education programme for Primary School Teachers issued in 2021: interpersonal; pedagogical; didactic; organisational; team collaboration; collaboration with local community; reflection and professional development. Specific indicators during initial professional education depend on three levels: qualified for training after year 1 (level 1), qualified for final traineeship (level 2) and qualified to start practising in schools (Bachelor level, level 3) (Singer/Romijn 2024).

This chapter has been able to illustrate only just some of the required and desired competences for early childhood core practitioners. At a general level, similarities can be found across countries and age-group specialisations. However, on closer examination, the question of what competences early childhood professionals need reveals a number of differences. This variance relates to the:

– Content and detail of competence statements
– Emphasis given to personal competences
– Priority given to different work tasks and the
– Specificity of competences for early childhood.

In terms of ECEC specificity, competence profiles for school-based pre-primary settings (in some part-integrated and all bi-sectoral ECEC systems) tend to show less early years orientation than those in unitary systems. They are often formulated for all teachers in the school system, implying that competence frameworks can vary in emphasis across different core practitioner types.

6.2 Curriculum in ECEC initial professional education: six country examples

As with most topics selected for closer analysis, both variance and similarities exist between the 33 SEEPRO-3 countries in terms of the core curriculum and main knowledge domains considered essential when preparing students for the early childhood education and care professions. Again, as in the previous chapter on competence requirements, we will focus on the initial professional education (IPE) curricula for prospective *core practitioners*. Along similar lines, we have chosen six countries which represent different European regions, different ECEC system types, varying formal qualification requirements and IPE institutions as well as different core practitioner profiles: *Austria, Bulgaria, Finland, Portugal, Serbia* and *Sweden*.

6.2.1 IPE curricula in two unitary ECEC systems: Finland and Sweden

The teacher education programmes in these two Nordic countries both offer ISCED level 6 courses for prospective Early Childhood Pedagogy Professionals, i.e. study programmes which focus explicitly on the years preceding primary school. In both countries, universities have a good deal of autonomy in the conceptualisation of their course programmes and the two we are presenting here are from the University of Helsinki (*Finland*) and the University of Gothenburg (*Sweden*). In both countries, students are prepared for work in ECEC centres (1–5 years) as well as compulsory pre-primary classes for 6 year-olds.

The University of Helsinki programme for 'Teachers in ECEC' lasts three years and students are awarded 180 ECTS credits at the end of it (Chydenius 2024). The new curriculum is structured according to five dimensions described as: language and communication studies; basic studies in education; intermediate studies in education; studies providing professional readiness for work in ECEC and pre-primary education; and optional study modules (see Box 3). Students can study for part of the degree in another European country through exchange programmes such as ERASMUS or NORDPLUS.

Box 3

Finland: Curricular course modules – 'Teacher in ECEC' study programme, University of Helsinki (180 ECTS credits)

1. Language and communication studies (15 ECTS credits) This foundational dimension focuses on communication and interpersonal skills as well as academic writing in the students' native language (usually Finnish), oral and written skills in the second national language (usually Swedish) at level B1 of the Common European

> Framework of Reference for Languages (CEFR), as well as academic and professional communication in English at CEFR level B2. Also included in this part of the study programme is a focus on digital skills, communicating as a teacher and compiling a personal study plan.
>
> 2. *Education, basic studies* (25 ECTS credits)
>   Initial Education studies includes modules on: social, cultural and philosophical foundations of education; psychology of learning and development; planning, implementation and assessment of teaching I; planning, implementation and assessment of teaching in ECEC; toddler pedagogy.
>
> 3. *Education, intermediate studies* (45 ECTS credits)
>   The second set of Education studies includes field practice and modules on: support for learning and wellbeing*; planning, implementation and assessment of teaching II*; integrated practice*; advanced practice period*; qualitative research methods I; quantitative research methods I; Bachelor's thesis. 10 ECTS credits are awarded for scientific methods in this set of intermediate studies.
>
> 4. *Studies providing professional readiness for work in institutional early childhood education and pre-primary education* (60 ECTS credits)
>   The core part of the curriculum, making up one third of the total study time with 60 ECTS credits focuses specifically on pedagogy and learning areas in early childhood and includes the following modules: preschool and pre-primary education; activity learning in early childhood education; diversity of development and early childhood special education; mathematics pedagogy; environmental education and primary science; pedagogy of language and interaction; moral and worldview education; children's literature and drama; visual arts education; music education; pedagogy of handicraft; pedagogy of physical education.
>
> 5. *Optional study modules* (35 ECTS credits)
>   For example: special education; pre-primary and early primary years education.

* Teachers working in comprehensive schools (primary and secondary schools) and other educational institutions must have 60 ECTS credits in *Pedagogical Studies for Teachers*, 35 of which can be obtained in the Bachelor's programme for teachers in ECEC.
Source: Chydenius 2024

Within the framework of national Higher Education legislation, universities in *Sweden* with a teacher education specialisation are free to choose their preferred curricular areas and study approaches. The University of Gothenburg offers a programme for *förskollärare* (lit. Preschool Teachers) with 210 ECTS credits and a duration of seven semesters (which can be extended to 4 years). The course is organised into three main knowledge domains: educational sciences; preschool pedagogy; and work placement (see Box 4). Education for sustainable development is a core dimension at the University of Gothenburg and a distinctive feature throughout the programme (Karlsson Lohmander 2024).

Box 4
Sweden: Curricular course modules – 'Preschool Teacher' study programme, University of Gothenburg (210 ECTS credits)

1. *Educational sciences* (60 ECTS credits) This knowledge domain comprises seven integrated and overlapping themes: history, governance, conditions and founding values – including democracy and human rights – of preschool and school; curriculum theory and didactics; theory of science, research methodology; an interdisciplinary perspective on development and learning including cognitive science and special education; social relations, conflict resolution and leadership; follow-up and analysis of learning and development for Preschool Teachers; evaluation and developmental work. 2. *Preschool pedagogy (subject studies)* (120 ECTS credits) This core curricular area includes subject-related didactics within the domain of early childhood education (105 ECTS credits) and a degree project/dissertation (15 ECTS credits). It comprises six themes: children's play, communication, language and literacy; children's mathematical learning; play, learning, and care; co-operation with guardians, the preschool class, the school-age *educare* setting and the school; aesthetic learning processes; nature, environment and technology. In the final semester, there are two course modules at advanced level comprising 15 ECTS credits each. One is compulsory (sustainable development and global perspectives) and one is an optional in-depth specialisation focusing on one of the themes above. 3. *Work placement – practicum, 20 weeks* (30 ECTS credits) Field practice through a supervised work placement is organised as four distinctive course modules.

Source: Karlsson Lohmander 2024

6.2.2 IPE curricula in two part-integrated ECEC systems: Austria and Serbia

While in *Austria*, initial professional education for prospective 'Early Childhood Pedagogues' takes place at tertiary-level Vocational Colleges for Early Childhood Pedagogy, where award holders leave with an ISCED 5 level qualification and a professional profile as an Early Childhood Pedagogy Professional, in *Serbia*, prospective 'ECEC Teachers' study at Colleges and Academies of Applied Studies or University faculties and gain a qualification at ISCED 6 or ISCED 7 level with a Pre-primary Education Professional profile for work with children from 3 up to 7 years of age.

In *Austria*, the five-year short-cycle tertiary vocational course of studies (with no ECTS credits) is divided into three main parts: general education subjects; theoretical and field-based studies; creative arts and movement education, as shown in Box 5 (Krenn-Wache 2024).

Box 5
Austria: Curricular content distribution – 'Early Childhood Pedagogue' vocational programme

1. General education subjects Around 40% of the course comprises general education subjects required for the completion of the school-leaving examination (*Matura*), i.e. the general university entrance requirement. The 13 subject areas are: German; English; history; social studies; political education; geography and economics; applied mathematics; physics; chemistry; biology and ecology (including physiological foundations, health, nutrition); applied sciences; nutrition with hands-on practice and the basics of computer science. **2. Theoretical and field-based studies** Roughly one third of the curriculum is focused on theoretical and field-based studies. These include: pedagogy (with psychology and philosophy); inclusive education; didactics; practicum; organisation, management and legislation (including scientific work); communication practice and group dynamics. Roughly half of this time (15%) is spent on field practice. **3. Creative arts and movement education** In Austria, a particular emphasis is placed on the creative arts and on movement education. This curricular area makes up roughly 27% of the overall curriculum throughout the five years. It includes both general and occupation-related content and competences in the following areas: visual arts education; handicraft education; textile design; music education; voice training, elocution; Instrumental studies; music and movement; movement education and Sport.

Source: Krenn-Wache 2024

In *Serbia*, 16 higher education institutions offer both Bachelor and Master level IPE programmes for prospective ECEC Teachers, which are categorised as either 'applied studies' or 'academic studies'. The ECEC Workforce report from *Serbia* has drawn together a selection of the curricular content of these varying courses across the country (Miskeljin 2024). Box 6 presents examples of the curricular focus in the study programmes for a Bachelor's degree, which is the minimum qualification requirement for ECEC Teachers in Serbia.

Box 6
Serbia: Curricular content of Bachelor-level programmes for prospective ECEC Teachers (selection)

Bachelor applied studies
Compulsory subjects are structured according to four areas: **1. Academic general** General pedagogy: preschool pedagogy; general psychology; developmental psychology; psychology of childhood and adolescence; inclusive pedagogy; Serbian language and communication; children's literature; professional identity; philosophy; foreign language; ethics; ICT in early education; health education; physical and medical education. **2. Theoretical-methodological** Organisation and structure of the educational process; introduction to scientific work; methodology of pedagogy research; integrated preschool curriculum; integrative approach to educational content; children's play.

3. *Scientific, e.g. artistic-professional*
Sociology of childhood; anthropology of childhood; visual arts; music; kinesiology; drama in education; vocal-instrumental teaching; orchestra.
4. *Professional applicative*
Methods of arts education; methods of speech development; methods of environmental education; methods of music education; methods of physical education; methods of initial mathematical concepts.
Elective subjects include:
Art workshop; child and computer; visual culture; games workshop; drama workshop; preschool as an open system; inclusion of socially deprived children; pedagogical documentation; child subculture; teamwork; models of preschool teacher professional development.
Bachelor academic studies
Compulsory subjects (selection).
1. *Academic general*
General pedagogy; general psychology; Serbian language and communication; foreign language; preschool pedagogy; developmental psychology; family pedagogy; inclusive pedagogy; philosophy; health education; physical and medical education; philosophy of education.
2. *Theoretical-methodological*
Pedagogy/didactics; theory of education; basics of methodology of pedagogical research; pedagogical methodology; research in pedagogy; action research in preschool education; methodology of qualitative and quantitative pedagogical research.
3. *Scientific, e.g. artistic-professional*
Sociology; visual arts; music; kinesiology; drama in education; vocal-instrumental teaching; orchestra; vocal-instrumental practicum.
4. *Professional applicative*
Didactics of art activities; preschool didactics; methods of arts education; methods of speech development; methods of environmental education; methods of music education; methods of physical education; methods of initial mathematical concepts.
Elective subjects include: Ethics; ICT in early education; media education; culture of speech and communication, fundamentals of natural sciences and ecology; play and dance; puppet and stage art; multimedia techniques in education.

Source: Miskeljin 2024

6.2.3 *IPE curricula in two bi-sectoral ECEC systems: Bulgaria and Portugal*

In both *Bulgaria* and *Portugal*, ministerial responsibility for ECEC is split according to the children's age.[14] In this section we look at the IPE curricula for professionals working in kindergartens under the responsibility of the Ministry

---

14 According to the Bulgarian ECEC Workforce Profile report, policy discussions have been taking place regarding the integration of the two sectors currently under Health (nursery provision 0–2 years) and Education (kindergartens 3–6 years) into a unified ECEC system. (Engels-Kritidis 2024).

of Education for children from 3 years of age up to primary school entry, whereby in both countries qualified teachers may also work in nursery settings with younger children.

In *Bulgaria*, each university with a faculty of education develops its own curriculum according to minimum teacher qualification requirements set out in a national government directive. 'Pre-primary Teachers' working with 3 to under 7 year-olds have a Bachelor-level ISCED 6 qualification and award holders have a Pre-primary and Primary Education Professional profile. The study programme lasts four years and students are awarded 240 ECTS credits. Although optional, it is common for Pre-primary Teachers to have a Master's degree. They also have the possibility of working in a coordinating role across different nursery settings where the core group-leading practitioners are Medical Nurses (also an ISCED 6 level qualification) (Engels-Kritidis 2024).

In *Portugal*, a regulatory framework for the IPE of early childhood professionals is similarly set out at national level – in a Decree Law. 'Early Childhood Teachers' are qualified at ISCED 7 level and complete a three-year Bachelor's degree in Basic Education followed by a three-semester Master's degree in Pre-School Education (Araújo 2024). Their professional profile is that of an Early Childhood Pedagogy Professional and they can work in ECEC settings across the early childhood age range.

At Sofia University St. Kliment Ohridski in *Bulgaria*, there are two relevant study programmes. One is the four-year course in Pre-school and Primary School Pedagogy, which qualifies for work with 3 to 11 year-olds in kindergartens and primary schools; the other is the Pre-school Pedagogy with a Foreign Language programme. The first comprises 2,850 academic hours in 58 curricular areas; the second comprises 2,475 hours of study and 45 curricular areas. Both have to comply with the mandatory requirements set out by the government in the six areas shown in Table 18.

Table 18
Bulgaria: Mandatory courses for qualifying as a Pre-primary Teacher (240 ECTS credits)

	Academic course	Minimum duration in academic hours
1	Pedagogy	60 (min. 30 hours of lectures)
2	Main specialisation course: preschool pedagogy	45 (min. 15 hours of lectures)
3	Psychology	60 (min. 30 hours of lectures)
4	Didactics/tuition methodology	120 (min. 30 hours of lectures)
5	Inclusive education	30
6	Information and communication technology in education; working in a digital environment	30

Source: Bulgarian government Directive for State Requirements for Attainment of the Professional Qualification of 'Teacher', dated 11.11.2016 and last updated on 05.02.2021

Both study programmes include the following curricular content: basics of Education; didactics, history of pedagogy and Bulgarian education; pedagogical psychology; preschool pedagogy; pedagogy of early childhood (0–3 years); pedagogy of play in early childhood; pedagogical assessment; basics of primary school education; children's literature; pedagogy of language use and speech development; pedagogy of child-environment interaction; pedagogy of mathematics; pedagogy of music; pedagogy of art; pedagogy of movement. The theoretical studies end with written state exams (Engels-Kritidis 2024).

In *Portugal*, the prescribed IPE components (for all teachers across the education system) are shown in Table 19, together with the number of ECTS credits awarded for each of the four dimensions. An additional 'cultural, social and ethical' dimension does not have formally allocated ECTS credits but can be integrated where appropriate. Each higher education institution has 10 ECTS that can be freely allocated to the components, as long as they respect the established minimum.

Table 19
Portugal: Prescribed curricular elements in the IPE of Early Childhood Teachers

Education/ training components	Minimum ECTS credits per component		
	Bachelor in Basic Education	Master in Pre-school Education	Master in Pre-School and Primary Education
Teaching subject	125	6	18
General education	15	6	6
Subject-specific didactics	15	24	36
Initiation into professional practice	15	41	54

Source: Portuguese Decree-Law 79 (2014), in: Araújo 2024

The particular focus of the Bachelor in Basic Education is on the knowledge needed for *teaching* in certain content areas or disciplines. The distribution of the 125 ECTS credits prescribed by law is as follows: Portuguese (30 ECTS credits); mathematics (30 ECTS credits); natural sciences; history and geography of Portugal (30 ECTS credits); expressive arts (music, visual arts, drama); and physical/motor expression (30 ECTS credits). The HEI is free to allocate the remaining 5 ECTS credits to selected content areas. The integration of field practice varies, with some institutions offering observation and cooperation experiences throughout the three years and others tending to provide these experiences only in the final year of the course. In the courses at Master's level, subject-specific didactics (in mathematics, spoken language and basics of writing; natural and social sciences; aesthetic education; physical education) and, in particular, supervised educational practice constitute the core curricular elements (Araújo 2024).

6.2.4 Distinctive features of curricular content in the six countries

Across these six country examples, a number of distinctive features of the IPE curricula designed for prospective ECEC core practitioners have become visible.

The outstanding element in the prescribed components of the IPE curricular framework in *Bulgaria* is the attention given to inclusive education and information and communication technologies (ICT) in education. As elaborated in the section on the ECEC curricula in Part I of this book, digital education remains in general a neglected area in ECEC.

In *Austria*, a special feature is the strong emphasis on the aesthetic dimension (creative arts) and movement. General education is also a key dimension of the Austrian IPE courses, since students are not only working towards a professional award but also a university entrance qualification.

In *Portugal*, there appears to be a primary focus on disciplines and didactics rather than the 'educational sciences' strongly emphasised in the *Swedish* study programme.

A special feature of the IPE programme in *Finland* is the inclusion of both quantitative and qualitative research methods in ECEC. Similarly, both the curricular frameworks in *Sweden* ('theory of science and research methodology') and *Serbia* ('action research in preschool education' and 'methodology of qualitative and quantitative pedagogical research') include the research knowledge dimension in Bachelor level courses as an important requisite for professionalism in early childhood education and care.

6.3 Field practice in the initial professional education of ECEC core practitioners

Requirements and modalities regarding supervised field practice during the initial professional education of core practitioners are regulated by national legislation in *Croatia, Denmark, Norway, Serbia, Spain*, in the education/school sectors in the *French Community of Belgium, Bulgaria, Czech Republic, Hungary, Italy, Poland, Portugal* and in the UK. In some countries they are specified in national level guidelines, as in France, or in agreements between the IPE institutions and the ECEC settings hosting the students, as in *Latvia*. Otherwise they are included in the curricular frameworks of the IPE institutions, as, for example, in *Austria, Cyprus, Romania* and *Switzerland*. In *Lithuania* (0–6) there are no national regulations on the role of field practice in the IPE of ECEC professionals, as is also the case in *Bulgaria, Hungary, The Netherlands* and *Poland* for the IPE of professionals working with children under the age of 3.

The *duration* of field-based studies varies greatly. Whereas in *Malta* (0–2) a traineeship for work in a childcare centre may last only five weeks, for prospective pedagogues in *Denmark* it amounts to a total of 15 months. In several countries, about one fifth of the study programme is dedicated to field practice, as is the case in *Greece* and *Spain*. The practice-based component of the IPE of (Early Childhood) Educators in *Germany*, who comprise the majority of ECEC staff, amounts to about one third of the three-year study programme at a vocational college for social pedagogy. About half of the 16 federal states have established an additive training model, i.e. a two-year, primarily theoretical and college-based component followed by a one-year work placement in an ECEC centre or other socio-pedagogical setting. Otherwise, within the framework of an integrated model, field practice takes place in a number of blocks spread over the entire study programme, as is the case in most European countries.

In the countries with an ISCED 6 level of initial professional education, there are marked differences between countries – but also within countries – in the allocation of *ECTS credits* for field practice assignments. In the university study programmes for prospective ECEC Teachers in *Croatia*, for example, the number of ECTS credits for field practice range from five to nine, meaning that in general the proportion is low. At the other end of the spectrum, up to 50 out of a total of 240 ECTS credits are awarded for the field practice component in the *Spanish* IPE programmes for candidate ECE Teachers.

Table 20 presents examples for different types of core professional in two unitary (*Denmark, Finland*), two part-integrated (*Italy, Spain*) and two bi-sectoral ECEC systems (*Greece, Poland*). For Finland, both types are included.

With over a third of ECTS credits assigned to field practice, *Denmark* is the country with the highest number of ECTS credits for this part of the study programme, whereas in *Poland*, for example, less than 5% of the five-year programme leading to an ISCED 7 qualification as Pre-primary and Primary School Teacher focuses on field practice in ECEC or primary school settings. In *Finland*, where two kinds of ECEC core professional are included in legislation, the length of field studies is higher in the study programmes at universities of applied sciences leading to the award of Social Pedagogue in ECEC than in the university courses for prospective Teachers in ECEC.

Table 20
Supervised field practice: ECTS credits awarded for total IPE and for field practice component in six countries

Country	Total IPE ECTS credits	Field practice ECTS credits	Proportion of IPE studies	Type of core professional / → SEEPRO professional profile
Denmark	210	75	35.7	Pedagogue 0–5 → Early childhood pedagogy professional
Finland	210	45	21.4	Social Pedagogue in ECEC 0–6 → Social and childhood pedagogy professional
Spain	240	50	20.8	ECE Teacher 0–5 → Early childhood pedagogy professional
Greece	240	46	19.2	Pre-primary Teacher 4–5 → Pre-primary education professional
Italy	300	24	8.0	Pre-primary Teacher 3–5 → Pre-primary and primary education professional
Finland	180	12–20	6.7–11.1	Teacher in ECEC 0–6 → Early childhood pedagogy professional
Poland	300	10	3.3	Kindergarten Teacher 3–5 → Pre-primary and primary education professional

Source: SEEPRO-3 country reports 2024, in: Oberhuemer/Schreyer 2024b

In terms of *content* and the *competences* to be acquired, the differences are not so marked. As a rule, trainees begin by observing everyday practice and the activities of experienced professionals; they then progress through planning, preparing and implementing specific activities under supervision; and finally there comes a phase of working independently. Core competences include transferring theoretical knowledge into practice and reflecting on their own role. This often includes keeping a portfolio or a work placement diary. In Sweden, this progression is termed as: *investigating, implementing* and *synthesising*, indicating gradually increasing complexity. The Swedish course modules relating to field practice are structured as shown in Box 7 (Karlsson Lohmander 2024).

Box 7
Field practice course modules: Sweden

> *Module 1, semester 1:* observing the overall organisation and everyday practice, with a focus on children's learning and own professional development. Investigating how the major steering documents, including curricular frameworks and theoretical perspectives, are implemented.
>
> *Module 2, semester 3:* didactic planning, implementation, and documentation of theme-oriented work with children integrating mathematics, language and communication.
>
> *Module 3, semester 4:* aims to develop knowledge and understanding of pedagogical leadership and its importance for social relationships and conflict management. The focus is on

> systematic approaches towards promoting children's development and learning, including aesthetic learning processes. Students are encouraged to gradually 'replace' the Preschool Teacher and take independent responsibility for planning and implementing different activities such as arts, drama, dance, and music with children and to collaborate with the work team and parents/guardians.
>
> *Module 4, semester 6:* focus on the importance of pedagogical leadership and the professional role to manage the complexity of preschool education from a societal and sustainable development perspective in relation to children's differing needs and sometimes unequal preconditions. Central to this module are children's perspectives and own pedagogical-didactical perspectives related to the curriculum.

In *Italy*, the organisation of field practice in the study programmes for Pre-primary and Primary School Teachers aims to create a productive interlinking of problem-centred knowledge acquisition at the university with the exploratory testing of applied knowledge in a real-life education setting. University staff known as 'organising tutors' are responsible for the overall cooperation between the university, the ECEC centres (or schools) and the Centre Leaders (or School Heads). 'Coordinating tutors' are responsible for leading and organising the work of the student mentors (who are called 'trainee tutors' in *Italy*). Both are experienced professionals on leave of absence from their regular workplace for four years. A university-based interdisciplinary commission develops the field practice programme on the basis of feedback from the student mentors. Regular workshops provide a space for ongoing planning and reflection (Picchio and Bove 2024).

The *student mentors* in the ECEC settings are usually required to have a specified amount of professional experience (e.g. five years in *Latvia, Lithuania, Portugal*). Overall, extra training is rarely required for taking on this position, although this is becoming more common: both *Finland* and *Sweden* offer a university course focusing on the mentoring role for which 5 ECTS and 7.5 ECTS, respectively, are awarded. In some countries, student mentors are remunerated for their supervision and guidance (e.g. in *Croatia* 0–5, *Denmark* 0–5, *France* 2–5, *Norway* 0–5 and *Romania* 3–5), but as a rule, no salary bonus is granted for this additional work.

In *Denmark*, where trainees spend a considerable amount of time in the practicum centres, the specific role of the *ECEC centre as a recognised site of initial professional education* has been included in a ministerial decree which highlights the role of the workplace setting in IPE. The host ECEC centre is required to develop a practicum concept which includes the following elements: a description of the setting, including its goals, the specific user group and the overall approach; a field practice education plan which aligns with the competence goals for the specific practicum period and includes suggestions for relevant literature, how student guidance is carried out and how collaboration with the university college is organised. The ECEC centre has to arrange a meeting with the university college and the student after two-thirds of the first, second and third practicum periods. Following this, the centre has to make a statement declaring how the student will be supported in achieving the competence goals for the practicum period in question (Bekendtgørelse – Danish Ministerial Decree 2017, § 9).

Traditionally the sole responsibility of the IPE institution, the example from *Denmark* represents a significant upgrading of the pivotal position of the ECEC setting in the initial professional education of core practitioners. Combined with transparent cooperation strategies and a consolidation of the mentoring role through designated posts of responsibility anchored in the organisational and pay structures, a framework can be established for a new 'culture of cooperation' (Oberhuemer 2015), in which both the IPE institution and the ECEC centre acknowledge their shared role and equal responsibility in supporting aspiring early childhood professionals.

7 Alternative routes into the ECEC professions – lateral entry

The marked shortage of staff in many countries is leading to a focus on the provision of alternative qualifying routes and opportunities for lateral entry into the ECEC field. It is envisaged that, under certain conditions and without undermining the overall staffing quality, people without the regular core professional qualification can be included in the ECEC centre team. Among stakeholders, however, voices are being raised that address the potential risks of such an approach. One example from the federal state of Bavaria in *Germany* criticises the slimmed down core content and the lack of assessment procedures at the federal state level in the new modular training for career changers (Binder 2024).

In some SEEPRO-3 countries (e.g. *Croatia, Estonia, Hungary, Italy, Poland, Portugal* or *Serbia*), people without regular or relevant training who wish to work as an early childhood professional only have the option of completing a full course of regular initial professional education. In *Ukraine*, people without the appropriate qualifications can only take on the position of a technical assistant, who can only perform non-pedagogical tasks under the supervision of the group leader. In other countries, however, there are various options for lateral entry. These are presented in three categories below: via special training models, through additional qualifying courses and via the recognition of existing qualifications or (informal) competences.

Specialised lateral entry models can be found in some countries and either build on existing qualifications, including non-relevant qualifications, or lead to a qualification through a CPD pathway.

In *Denmark*, for example, academically qualified persons with a non-relevant Bachelor's degree can take advantage of the so-called 'track change model' to become a Pedagogue in the early childhood field. Refugees from non-western countries who have a university degree can also obtain the necessary qualifications by completing a 12-month course at a university college. The severe shortage of qualified staff in *Germany* has led to new IPE formats emerging which are offered alongside the traditional qualifying routes in the field. Overall, a pluralisation of formats can be observed, in particular dualised, work-integrated and remunerated qualification pathways for (E)CEC trainees. Due to the simultaneity of paid work and qualification, those following such a pathway can be included in the staffing ratio. However, this practice is seen critically by field experts, as the trainees are not yet fully-fledged professionals. In *Romania* 3-5, specialists with a teaching qualification in non-educational areas, who therefore work as 'unqualified' staff, can qualify as a Pre-primary and

Primary School Teacher through so-called modular 'reconversion programmes'. There is a whole range of different options in the *Czech Republic*, including a combination of training and studies; an additional baccalaureate-type examination in early childhood education for candidates with a secondary school leaving certificate; or, in the event of acute staff shortages, the (temporary) recruitment of people over the age of 55 and with more than 20 years of professional kindergarten experience as a core practitioner.

Lateral entry via an additional qualifying course is a further option for interested persons with non-relevant qualifications, as is the case in *Lithuania, Russia* and *Slovenia*. In *Sweden*, too, teachers (including early childhood education core pedagogues) who do not have a regular teaching qualification can acquire this through an additional course. In the *United Kingdom*, beginners without any qualifications receive in-house training, or EQF level 4 (ISCED 3) core practitioners can achieve higher qualifications through internships and remote learning options. In the 'Baobab project' of the *Flemish Community of Belgium*, people with a migrant background who work as assistants are able to gain qualifications at a university of applied sciences alongside their work.

A third option for lateral entry is the *recognition of prior learning and acquired competences*. In *Finland*, staff with an upper secondary education can acquire a vocational qualification as an ECEC Nurse, Children's Instructor or Special Needs Assistant by following a route based partially or solely on competences and which can then be recognised as equivalent to a regular qualification. Similarly, in the childcare sector in *Malta*, persons without formal qualifications can have their informal skills assessed via the so-called trade testing system. In the *Flemish Community of Belgium*, non-qualified staff in the childcare sector can participate in an assessment organised by a recognised test centre or by a Centre for Adult Education, where non-formal and informal learning experiences of the applicant are validated. In the *French Community of Belgium*, it is possible to shorten the duration of studies for trainee Pre-primary Teachers by assessing previously acquired competences. Individual competences are also recognised in *The Netherlands* within the qualifying courses as a Childcare Worker. In the childcare sector in *France*, qualification requirements can be partially replaced through professional experience or the validation of acquired competences – not, however, in the case of the Paediatric Nurses who act as Centre Leaders. In *Luxembourg*, both in the non-formal and formal education sectors, qualifications acquired in *Belgium* and *Switzerland* are recognised, as is relevant professional experience. In the play work, health care and social care sectors in *Wales* and *Scotland* (*UK*), it is relatively easy to change careers, as many compulsory subjects in training are the same and are mutually recognised.

Overall, however, *permeability between sectors* with regard to the professional education and training of ECEC specialists is rather limited (e.g. *France, Hungary*) or non-existent (e.g. *Belgium, Greece, The Netherlands*). As a rule, it is assumed that professionals who wish to switch to the other sector will adapt their existing training to the respective requirements by completing a full study programme. For countries with an integrated ECEC system (and also in the federal systems of *Austria* and *Germany*), the question of permeability between sectors or within them does not arise, as core professionals can work with children of all age groups.

8 Continuing professional development in the early childhood field

A number of European research studies indicate that continuing professional development (CPD) in the field of early childhood education and care is more effective if it is orientated towards the current qualification needs of staff and is carried out on a regular, supervised and long-term basis (CARE 2015; Eurofound 2015; Sharmahd et al. 2017; Jensen/Iannone 2018). However, the framework conditions for CPD for core ECEC professionals vary greatly in the countries of the SEEPRO-3 study. This chapter provides a brief overview of legislation and regulation, providers and main forms of CPD, the possible obligation to participate in CPD activities and current key topics, presenting some country examples for each. The concluding section indicates the overall lack of supportive conditions for assistant staff.

8.1 Legislation and regulatory frameworks

In eight of the ten countries with a *unitary* ECEC system, the continuing professional development of core practitioners is regulated by national legislation and frameworks. *Norway* and *Sweden* are the only countries where this is not the case; here the responsibility, organisation and administration of CPD lies with the local authorities.

Although there is currently no nationally coherent and transparent system of further education and training for the early childhood sector in *Sweden*, a national performance and qualification system for head teachers, school teachers and Early Childhood Teachers will be introduced from 2025 with the aim of strengthening and developing skills, facilitating career advancement and making the teaching profession fundamentally more attractive (Karlsson Lohmander 2024: 1741).

In *Croatia*, strengthening the professional development and training opportunities of staff working in the education system – including ECEC professionals and centre managers – is one of the goals of the National Development Strategy of the Republic of Croatia until 2030 (Croatian Official Gazette, No. 30/2021). However, these goals are not yet enshrined in the latest Early Childhood Education Act (2023), which does not include any criteria for implementation of the Strategy goals in the ECEC field.

With the exception of the childcare sectors 0–2 in *Malta* and *Romania*, CPD is also regulated by law in countries with a *part-integrated* ECEC system. In those with federal structures such as *Austria* and *Germany*, however, these regulations differ depending on the federal state and the provider. In the four UK nations (*England, Wales, Scotland, Northern Ireland*) of the devolved ECEC system, statutory frameworks relating to CPD only apply to ECEC teachers working in the state education system, but not to staff in the private, voluntary and independent non-state sector.

In countries with a *bi-sectoral* ECEC system, CPD is usually enshrined in legislation by way of decrees or framework regulations. Here, however, there may be significantly less favourable regulations for the childcare sectors compared to the education sectors. In *Poland*, for example, regulations for the continuing professional development of nursery staff working with under 3 year-olds are not specified in any way in the current legislation for the childcare sector, and an entitlement to a specific number of days for professional development is not guaranteed in their contracts. By way of contrast, the rights and obligations of Pre-primary Teachers working in public sector kindergartens for 3 to under 7 year-olds are regulated by a Teachers' Charter (1982), which, among other things, secures funding for CPD at the national, regional and municipal levels of the education system. At the municipal level, funds amounting to 1% of the planned annual expenditure on teachers' salaries are made available for CPD measures, and the distribution of these funds must be coordinated with the teachers' unions (Żytko et al. 2024: 1283).

8.2 Providers and main forms of continuing professional development

Continuing professional development is offered by national educational institutions and regional training institutes as well as by ECEC provider associations, university departments, research institutes, municipal networks or accredited private and civil society organisations/associations, depending on the structures that have developed in the respective country. They take the form of seminars, courses, thematic conferences, workshops, certification training and weekend courses as well as in-house sessions in the ECEC centres, longer-term study courses, stays abroad and self-education.

A national survey conducted with a representative sample in 2020 in *Croatia* revealed the following picture: the most common form of professional development for ECEC professionals, mentioned by 82.5% of respondents, took place in the ECEC setting through colloquia and learning communities; in second place (52.3%) were training courses or conferences organised by the National Agency for Education and Teacher Training and in third place (50.2%) were professional development courses paid for or offered by the employer (50.2%). The smallest number of respondents (27.0%) took part in a self-funded professional development programme. However, a quarter of staff had not attended any kind of CPD during the previous year (Matković et al. 2020; Bouillet 2024: 223).

8.3 Continuing professional development as an entitlement and a duty

According to Eurydice indicators (2023), CPD measures for ECEC staff are defined as *mandatory*, with a time specification; as *optional*, without a legal obligation; as a *legal entitlement*; or as a *professional duty,* without a more precise specification (European Commission/EACEA/Eurydice 2023: 15).

In the 33 SEEPRO-3 countries, both the obligation to attend certain courses or events and the legal entitlement to a regulated and paid number of hours or days of further education and training per year vary greatly. As a rule, compulsory CPD is free of charge for professionals.

With the exception of *Norway*, where CPD is always voluntary, there are a number of mandatory measures in the *unitary* ECEC systems, even if there is no statutory obligation to participate in CPD in *Denmark* and *Sweden* (European Commission/EACEA/Eurydice 2023: 15). These are mostly focused on the implementation of new curricular requirements or other innovations (*Denmark, Lithuania, Slovenia, Sweden*).

In terms of requirements for participation in CPD, these are, for example, 36 hours within a period of three years in *Latvia* and 120 hours within five years in *Ukraine*, while in *Slovenia* core practitioners, assistant early childhood staff and centre managers the requirement is five days per year. In *Denmark* and *Sweden* there is no prescribed number of hours; in *Estonia* up to 30 days/year can be taken on request.

In countries with a *part-integrated* ECEC system, CPD is also at least partially compulsory, for example, if it is requested by the employer, or for professionals in state pre-primary schools 3–5 in *Italy*. In *Germany*, only in the federal states of Mecklenburg-Western Pomerania and Thuringia is participation in CPD mandatory for a specified number of days.

With regard to the time entitlement for CPD, core staff over the entire ECEC phase in *Serbia*, for example, are entitled to 60 hours per year, around two days per year in *Austria* and 270 hours every five years in *Romania*, while the entitlement in *Luxembourg* differs according to the specific education sector, with 32 hours of entitlement every two years for staff in the non-formal sector 0–3 (European Commission/EACEA/Eurydice 2023: 15).

In the *bi-sectoral* ECEC systems, the obligation and time entitlement to CPD also varies. In the education sector 3–5 in *Slovakia*, where professionals are entitled to at least five paid days, CPD is described as "both an entitlement and an obligation." Core professionals are also entitled to a further five working days' leave to prepare for and take the first and second certification exams needed for career advancement and a further five working days to take part in a kindergarten management module. A one-year unpaid sabbatical with a job guarantee upon return can also be authorised by the provider/employer (Miňová et al. 2024: 1566).

It is usually the providers or Centre Leaders who decide on the obligation, which is sometimes only for certain groups of staff. An example: in the education sector in the *French Community of Belgium*, six half days are compulsory for core professionals, whereas there is no obligation for assistants to participate in CPD.

Above all, the entitlement to CPD varies considerably, particularly in the childcare sectors of the bi-sectoral systems. For example, core professionals working with under 3 year-olds in *Hungary* are entitled to 10 to 15 days per year and in the *Czech Republic* to just eight hours. In the *Flemish Community of Belgium*, *France* and *Poland* there are no such entitlement regulations for the childcare sectors and in *Switzerland* they only exist for the canton of St. Gallen.

8.4 Participation in continuing professional development measures as a requirement for career promotion

Among the countries with a *unitary* ECEC system, one of the three criteria for the professional advancement of early childhood education staff in *Croatia* is participation in certain CPD courses. These include (a) seminars organised by the Ministry of Science and Education and (b) courses organised by professional organisations and associations. CPD participation contributes towards successfully applying for the position of Mentor, Councillor or (since 2022) Senior Councillor (Bouillet 2024: 222).

Similar promotion titles also exist in *Slovenia* 0–5 and *Serbia* 3–5. In Slovenia there is a highly structured system for gaining credit points by attending further education and training programmes or taking on special pedagogical tasks. Four promotion titles are awarded: Mentor, Advisor, Councillor and, since September 2023, Senior Councillor. The titles awarded are permanent and do not need to be reviewed or renewed. The required credits are defined in the collective agreement for the entire education sector and include participation in CPD, projects, expert conferences, publishing articles or organising events for children (Jager 2024: 1626).

In the education sector 3–5 in *Slovakia*, continuing professional development and training for teachers (including Pre-primary Teachers) is part of a career advancement system with four career levels: (a) novice/newly qualified teacher; (b) independent teacher; (c) teacher with first level of certification; (d) teacher with second level of certification. Within these levels, there are various positions such as head of a 'methods circle' or overall coordinator of the centre team (Miňová et al. 2024: 1567).

In *Germany*, there are currently no specific strategies or binding models for career advancement. However, a modular concept for CPD measures was developed as part of a study entitled 'Career Paths in ECEC' (Weßler-Poßberg et al. 2022). Examples include *horizontal* career paths (e.g. in the field of language, digital or inclusive education), *diagonal* career paths (e.g. positions as a student mentor or as a quality development officer) and *vertical* career paths (leadership/management of ECEC centres). Curricula have been developed for the qualifying modules (ten two-day blocks, half of which are self-study sessions). It is proposed that 20–30 ECTS credits be recognised for this advanced qualification (Oberhuemer/Schreyer 2024a: 647).

Beyond these specific career advancement options, all professionals can follow up their existing training with further regular qualifications or further and advanced training and in this way work, for example, as a language or support specialist (*Latvia*) or as a centre leader. In *Denmark*, for example, both municipal and private institutions have the opportunity to apply for funding for a model in which ECEC Pedagogues are trained for a position known as a 'professional beacon' (specially designated post) – either through three days of CPD or by completing a pedagogical diploma module (Jensen/Preus 2020). This new post is based on the idea that, in the spirit of distributed or collective management (Spring/Spring 2020), some management tasks are delegated to professionals within the centre. In the *Czech Republic*, professionals can qualify for higher positions such as pedagogues who guide newly qualified staff during their induction period or can become a school inspector through further education and training.

8.5 Current topics in CPD

Looking at the situation across countries, the range of topics in CPD activities is broad. Nevertheless, recurring focal points can be identified. These include: language and communication, digital education/technologies, supporting children with special educational needs, working with families – including refugee families, health issues, burnout syndrome and (for managers) ECEC centre management and leadership.

8.6 Availability of continuing professional development for ECEC assistant co-workers

In the majority of SEEPRO-3 countries, the core professionals are supported in their daily work by an ECEC Assistant (see chapter 5.3 for more details). In the childcare sectors in *Belgium*, the *Czech Republic*, *The Netherlands* and *Slovakia*, as well as in the education sectors in *Greece*, *Italy* and *Malta*, no assistant staff are deployed. In *Croatia* 0–6, Assistants with a basic pedagogical training are assigned the task of working with children with developmental delays.

In general, it can be stated that, compared with the conditions provided for core staff, CPD for assistant staff is barely regulated – if at all. While in the *Flemish Community of Belgium*, for example, every pre-primary setting 2½–5 is obliged to develop a CPD plan for core staff, assistant co-workers are very rarely included in these plans. However, an interesting example is reported from the *French Community of Belgium*: As part of the introduction of a new curriculum into pre-primary settings, an accompanying CPD course was organised for the first time for assistant staff. Although this was neither compulsory nor funded, over a third of the Assistants took part in the training, which is a positive indicator of their motivation to learn (Pirard et al. 2024: 110).

In *Germany*, providing CPD for ECEC Assistants is generally the responsibility of the respective employer, i.e. the setting provider. In the federal state of Bavaria, a nine-month qualifying programme is offered for ECEC Assistants (Childcarers) and other staff with a pedagogy-related qualification who wish to become core practitioners. The programme is followed by six months of guided field practice in order to gain the title of 'Pedagogical specialist in (E)CEC centres' (Oberhuemer/Schreyer 2024a: 642). There are also further training programmes in the *Czech Republic* for persons wishing to become Pedagogical Assistants, or in *Denmark* for Pedagogical Assistants who wish to qualify as a core professional. Otherwise, the SEEPRO-3 reports only rarely mentioned CPD programmes specifically for ECEC Assistants.

9 Newly qualified and newly appointed staff: Support measures in the workplace

In the SEEPRO-3 countries with a *unitary* ECEC system, newly qualified professionals are generally supported in a variety of ways at the start of their careers. One of these is the support from a mentoring specialist who is placed alongside the new professional (e.g. in *Estonia, Latvia, Norway, Sweden, Slovenia, Ukraine*). In *Finland*, the main focus is on peer counselling and support. A regulated probationary period is usually stipulated by law – for example, for 12 months in *Croatia, Lithuania, Sweden* and *Ukraine*.

One example: In *Sweden*, the ECEC Director is responsible for hiring specially qualified mentors to support novice professionals. These mentors are trained ECEC or Primary Teachers with relevant professional experience who are required to complete a nationally organised online course (7.5 ECTS). They accompany the new staff throughout the induction phase and sometimes beyond and provide them with professional, personal and social support as well as strengthening their understanding of ECEC centres as workplaces and their role in society (Karlsson Lohmander 2024).

In four of the ten countries with a *part-integrated* ECEC system, support for new professionals is not regulated by law and depends on the provider or the Centre Leader (*Austria, Germany, Russia*) or on the available finances (*Romania*). In the legally regulated induction programme in *Serbia*, on the other hand, mentoring specialists accompany the new professionals (for one or two years) until they are ready to take the licensing examination. In the *United Kingdom*, the regulations in *Scotland* are more detailed than in the other three nations due to a National Standard; however, all childcare facilities in the UK are required to offer an induction programme for newly appointed staff, in which they are accompanied by supervising or mentoring professionals who assess their CPD needs and evaluate their performance. In *Italy*, a probationary year is provided for professionals in the *scuole dell'infanzia*, during which a certain number of training courses or workshops are attended. In *Spain*, induction regulations differ depending on the provider: in public early childhood centres, newly qualified professionals are accompanied by experienced professionals during their first year of work and this phase concludes with an examination; in private subsidised ECEC centres, the probationary period lasts only four months and in private non-subsidised centres only three months. In *Luxembourg*, the regulations in the formal education sector are different to those in the non-formal sector, with the introductory phase being less regulated in the latter. In *Malta*, there is no regulated support system for new employees.

Support measures for newly qualified staff in countries with *a bi-sectoral* ECEC system often differ depending on whether they work with under 3 year-olds or over 3 year-olds. In *Belgium (French Community), Greece, Hungary, Ireland, Poland* and *Switzerland*, for example, no induction measures are provided for newly employed professionals in the childcare sectors; in the *Flemish Community of Belgium* and in *France*, modalities depend on the provider. Newly employed professionals who work with over 3 year-olds (or in *Switzerland* over 4 year-olds) in pre-primary education can generally benefit from various support measures, such as mentoring (e.g. in *Bulgaria, Hungary, Poland, Slovakia, Switzerland*). Although there are no on-site mentoring specialists in pre-primary schools in *Greece*, introductory training sessions are held during the first two years of employment. In *Portugal*, all professionals across both sectors are accompanied by experienced staff for a one-year probationary period; in *Hungary*, the induction period lasts two years. In the *Czech Republic*, a mentoring system has been trialled in the education sector since September 2023 with mentoring specialists, including job shadowing, consultations and CPD sessions. In *Cyprus*, new professionals can choose to attend courses from the regular CPD programme, but there are no specific support measures.

Part III

Reform initiatives – workforce and ECEC system challenges

10 Staff-related policy initiatives and reform strategies

The SEEPRO-3 cooperation partners were asked to report on relevant national initiatives or reform strategies related to the professionalisation and working conditions of ECEC staff. A selection of the innovations considered essential from a country expert perspective are summarised here under three main headings: (1) initiatives to improve initial professional education, (2) strategies to improve working conditions, including measures to combat staff shortages and (3) staff-related reforms as part of overall educational policy strategies.

10.1 Initiatives to improve initial professional education

A number of recent policy initiatives in various countries aim to improve the initial professional education (IPE) of ECEC core practitioners. In *Estonia*, for example, it is hoped that by adapting IPE more effectively to the national standards for the teaching profession that all ECEC core staff will have at least a BA degree and all centre leaders an MA degree in the not-too-distant future. Similarly, in *Ukraine,* the national professional standards adopted in 2021 for early childhood core practitioners and for centre leaders are being integrated into initial professional education courses and are used extensively in professional development activities (see chapter 5.2 for a detailed overview of the standards for centre leaders).

The findings of a government-commissioned evaluation in *Denmark* in 2020 suggest that a number of improvements are needed in the initial professional education of Pedagogues (*pædagoger*). It was noted, for example, that the objectives to be achieved in current courses are too numerous and the modules for conveying them unable to offer the in-depth knowledge needed. Another issue is that, while the lengthy field practice remains an essential and important part of IPE, the links between university colleges and practicum institutions are still not sufficiently clarified (Danish Agency for Higher Education and Science 2021; Koch/Jensen 2024: 404).

In *Austria*, the federal initiative 'Elementar+' opens up new ways for those already employed in nurseries or kindergartens as an Assistant to obtain a fully-fledged qualification as a core practitioner, i.e. as an Early Childhood Pedagogue. The three-year course based at the University of Graz is conceptualised as a regionally organised part-time programme, thus enabling participants to combine it with working in an ECEC setting. Also in *Austria*, the entry requirement aptitude tests for the regular initial professional education of core practitioners at tertiary-level vocational colleges have been changed from having to pass four examinations to a general assessment of the candidate's contact and communication abilities (Krenn-Wache 2024: 33).

In the childcare sector of the *French Community of Belgium*, a new Bachelor's degree course in early education has been introduced and a new CPD course for centre leaders. A revised profile is currently being developed both for professionals trained at upper secondary level and for initial professional education as a whole (Pirard et al. 2024: 118).

New study programmes specifically related to inclusion, multilingualism and digital skills have been introduced in *Slovakia*. In *Sweden,* there is also a move to focus more on the digital competence of staff in the early childhood education sector in initial professional education.

The recently issued, government approved document in *Russia* on 'Concept for the training of pedagogical staff for the education system for the period up to 2030' sets out professional standards for education staff in general, including core practitioners and Centre Leaders in kindergartens, and defines tasks, entry requirements to the profession (higher or secondary vocational education) and the required skills and knowledge (Volkova 2024: 1446).

In a few SEEPRO-3 countries, the minimum formal qualification for ECEC professionals has been raised. In *Poland*, for example, the minimum qualification for teachers in kindergartens (3–6) and primary schools was raised to Master's level in 2017. For 'Kindergarten Educators I and II' in *Malta*, who work with 3 and 4 year-olds, the minimum qualification requirement was raised from EQF level 4 to EQF level 5 in 2021.

In *Norway* and *Slovenia,* plans to reform the initial professional education routes have been announced, but have yet to be implemented.

10.2 Strategies to improve working conditions and measures to combat staff shortages

In a number of countries, reforms and initiatives have taken place to improve the working conditions of ECEC staff – mostly in relation to salary increases or other financial incentives. In *Estonia*, the aim is to achieve equal pay for early childhood professionals and primary school teachers; so far this is only the case in the two major cities, Tallinn and Tartu.

Over the past few years, salaries have also been increased in *Poland* (for career beginners), in *Sweden* (through the 'Salary boost for teachers' initiative) and in *Slovenia* (for Early Childhood Assistant Teachers). In the *Czech Republic*, a gradual increase in teachers' salaries (including those who work in kindergartens) is taking place, which should ultimately amount to 130% of the average salary). In *Wales (UK)*, financial support for low-skilled workers is being used to attract more potential qualified staff and in *Ireland's* non-school sector, it is hoped that a new core funding model will also lead to better pay and working conditions for professionals.

Various other measures are being taken to counter the prevailing staff shortage in many countries: in *Lithuania*, for example, students of education receive a scholarship if they commit to working in an ECEC centre after completing their studies. In *Latvia*, non-specialist graduates from universities of applied sciences and universities can work in ECEC centres even without additional training if they are accompanied by mentors. In *Finland*, a new publicity campaign aims to make the ECEC profession more attractive. In *France* and *Spain*, changes in the requirements for vocational qualifications, such as lowering the entry age, are intended to motivate more young people to show interest in working in the early childhood field. In general, however, it is always necessary to weigh up the risk of de-professionalisation or decline in quality which such measures tend to imply.

10.3 Staff-related reforms as part of overall educational policy strategies

A number of countries have adopted long-term national education policy strategies which also include staff-related reforms. Some examples are presented here.

- The 2021–2035 Education Strategy in Estonia sets out principles, goals, indicators and targets for all levels of the education system, as well as specific goals for the ECEC sector. These primarily emphasise the need for competent and motivated early childhood education professionals and leaders, as well as a stimulating learning environment and a child-centred approach to education. Three indicators are formulated: the subjective well-being of children and professionals; mastery of the Estonian language; and a participation rate of 95% of children aged 3 years to school entry by 2035, compared to the starting point of 92% in 2021 (Veisson/Peterson 2024: 449).
- The National Development Plan for the education system until 2027 in *Croatia* includes a strategy to increase the number of early childhood educators and support staff with specialist qualifications, such as psychologists or speech and language therapists, as well as a demand that they receive more support (Bouillet 2024: 226).
- In the *Czech Republic*, the Education Strategy 2030+ has also made it possible for career changers to enter the kindergarten profession. Further inno-

vations here relate to the new positions of so-called 'induction' and 'accompanying' teachers. The former support newly qualified staff during their probationary period as a kindergarten pedagogue and continuously evaluate their teaching, while the latter are responsible for supporting students during their field practice periods in kindergartens. In addition, a new competence profile has been created for university graduates with a specialisation in ECEC (Loudová Stralczynská 2024: 347f).
- In *Germany*, a number of initiatives also serve to improve the quality of the ECEC – with a particular focus on early education professionals (Oberhuemer/Schreyer 2024a: 652). The Professional Development Initiative for Early Childhood Educators (WiFF), which has been running since 2008, focuses on a multi-level approach towards professionalising the workforce and on interlinking vocational IPE and higher education IPE; the federal programme 'Staffing Campaign' (2019–2021) focused on the recruitment and retention of staff – as is the case with the most recent Overall Strategy for Professionals in Early Childhood and All-day Education and Care which was adopted in 2024 (BMFSFJ 2024). Current nationwide and state-specific data collections on the staffing situation are available in the Early Education Staffing Barometer compiled by the German Youth Institute.
- In *Italy*, the main focus of the reforms is the integration of the previously separate childcare sector into an 'integrated 0–6 system' as part of the national education system. Jointly accepted standards are being developed with regard to organisational and educational quality, and roles and responsibilities are being redefined. Among other things, 'Centres for 0–6 year-olds' (*poli per l'infanzia*) are being introduced with a new funding system (Picchio/Bove 2024: 899).
- The 0–2 cycle in *Spain* is to be strengthened as an educational cycle with its own pedagogical framework and regulated minimum requirements. Among other things, the aim is to compensate for the effects of cultural, social and economic inequalities on children's learning and to strengthen the early identification and implementation of support needs (Ancheta-Arrabal 2024: 1696).

11 Staff-related and system-related challenges from a country expert perspective

The cooperation partners from the SEEPRO-3 countries were asked to describe both staff-related and system-related *challenges* in their country. Understandably, these two perspectives tend to overlap. This chapter therefore presents a synopsis of the two focal points – personnel and system challenges – according to categories that were most often mentioned.

11.1 Staff shortages

The shortage of qualified staff across Europe is highly problematic – in two thirds (22) of the 33 SEEPRO-3 countries it is the most-cited challenge. This trend is confirmed in the European Commission's report on staff shortages (2024). The reports from *Bulgaria, Cyprus, Estonia, Hungary, Ireland, Italy, Latvia, Malta, Portugal, Russia* and *Spain* did not explicitly note a current shortage of core professionals or assistant co-workers, but in some it was expected in the near future (e.g. *Portugal*).

Worsening working conditions (e.g. in *Czech Republic, Denmark, Greece*) and/or the low status of the early childhood education professions (e.g. in *Estonia, Lithuania*) as well as low pay (e.g. in *Greece, Latvia, Slovakia, Ukraine*) are cited as reasons for staff shortages and the associated attempts at recruitment which deter potentially interested people from entering the profession. There are also reports of a continuing threat of staff shortages due to an ageing workforce (e.g. in *Greece, Romania* and *Slovakia*).

11.2 Staff to child ratios

Furthermore, in connection with the reported worsening of working conditions in ten countries, the inadequate ratio of qualified staff to children and the strain caused by working with increasingly large groups are particularly emphasised. Two examples:
- The ECEC system in *Sweden* was always internationally recognised for its good staff to child ratio. However, there are no national regulations on this, neither for ECEC centres nor for the (now compulsory) pre-school classes

for 6 year-olds. Municipalities are not obliged to follow the recommendations of the national education agency *Skolverket*. Recently, there has been a trend towards grouping 1 to 3 year-olds with 3 to 5 year-olds in order to 'increase flexibility' for children and professionals. However, these now rather large and more complex groups require clear structures and demand more organising tasks, possibly at the expense of ensuring that the children's wishes and influence are supported (Karlsson Lohmander 2024).

– Many ECEC centres in *Norway* lack the financial resources to meet the legal staffing requirements throughout the day. There are often fewer adults present than required, especially during off-peak hours. If most parents make full use of the childcare hours, this is often at the expense of the educational work with the children because fewer professionals are responsible for a greater number of children (Gulbrandsen 2024).

11.3 Initial professional education of core practitioners

For almost two thirds of the SEEPRO countries (19), challenges related to the *initial education of professionals* are mentioned. For example, the lack of definitions and regulations for prospective staff wishing to work with children under 3 years of age is criticised (e.g. in the *Czech Republic, France, Italy, Romania, Switzerland*). In *Romania*, the country report emphasises that it will be necessary to follow up the legislative integration of the under 3 year-olds into the Education system with a transparent conceptualisation of core staff qualification profiles and to develop complementary IPE courses.

The need for improved monitoring and regulating of the sometimes very different university study programmes which specialise in the IPE of ECEC professionals is also mentioned several times as a challenge for the higher education systems (e.g. *Croatia, Portugal*). A higher education qualification for all staff in ECEC centres is called for in *Estonia* so that the staffing challenges associated with the integration of all ECEC services under the responsibility of the Ministry of Education and Research can be adequately met. In *Finland*, the trend towards lowering admission criteria to IPE courses in order to solve staffing problems is viewed critically. In *Malta*, a critical point is that although a relatively new qualification at ISCED/EQF level 6 has been introduced for the ECEC field, it is not mandatory. The majority of ECEC staff have lower-level qualifications and there is currently no policy strategy for securing highly qualified core professionals.

11.4 Continuing professional development opportunities for centre leaders, core practitioners and assistant co-workers

More than a third of the country reports (13) highlight problems related to continuing professional development opportunities (see also chapter 8). In *Croatia*, for example, a more coordinated approach in terms of formats, programmes and topics is considered necessary in order to improve the quality and effectiveness of CPD. In *Spain*, the conditions for CPD depend heavily on the workplace. While participation in CPD measures for professionals in public ECEC institutions is both a right (with corresponding adjustment of working hours and reimbursement of costs) and even in some cases a reward (in terms of subsequent earnings or extra allowances), this is not the case for professionals employed in private ECEC centres. In the non-formal education sector in *Luxembourg*, an improved coordination of CPD is considered necessary in order to ensure that all staff are well-qualified, particularly important in this case since the workforce is highly heterogeneous in terms of social, linguistic and cultural background, qualifications, citizenship and place of residence. In *Malta*, CPD measures for childcare staff and managers working with under 3 year-olds are only offered on demand, which means that their opportunities to refresh or expand their knowledge continue to lag behind those of Kindergarten Educators working with 3 and 4 year-olds. In *Portugal*, it is noted that early childhood professionals are rarely included in large-scale national CPD programmes; moreover, CPD opportunities for the 0–2 sector, for assistants and for nursery managers need to be more strongly prioritised.

11.5 Integration at the ECEC system level

The reports from *Belgium, France, Luxembourg, The Netherlands* and *Hungary* – all except Luxembourg with fully bi-sectoral systems – emphasise the lack of coordination between the childcare and education sectors as a system-related challenge. Also, the country report authors from *Bulgaria, Greece* and *Portugal* expressly emphasise the need to pursue the goal of a unitary ECEC system, which is already under discussion in some cases.

Even in countries that have already taken the step of assigning all ECEC provision to *one* specific ministry at national level, in all cases to the Ministry of Education (see also chapter 2), considerable challenges still remain. Two examples:

- In *Italy*, the development of an integrated system from birth to 6 years is currently being driven forward following the provision of the legal basis. This poses a number of challenges, such as the provision of appropriate funding; ensuring accessibility to early education for all children; clarifying professional profiles, qualifications, functions and roles; creating a national monitoring system as well as revising the university curriculum for IPE to include work with under 3 year-olds (Picchio/Bove 2024).
- In order to improve the effectiveness of early education provision in *Luxembourg*, it is considered necessary to strengthen continuity between the non-formal (0 to under 4 year-olds) and formal sectors (4 and 5 year-olds), to identify similarities and differences between the pedagogical approaches in both and to ensure more equal opportunities, e.g. through the language skills acquired in early education and through positive attitudes towards languages (De Moll et al. 2024).

11.6 Equitable access to early childhood education and care settings

The experts in 17 countries see *equitable access for all children* to high-quality ECEC as well as the lack of places as a pressing problem that needs to be addressed more effectively through targeted policy measures. In addition to the insufficient number of places (e.g. in *Austria, Bulgaria*) and/or regional differences in availability (e.g. in *Lithuania, Poland*), the difficulty in accessing special groups of children, such as children with special educational needs (e.g. in *Denmark*) or children from Roma communities (e.g. in *Slovakia*), is emphasised. Another obstacle is the high expense of childcare for parents in some countries (e.g. in *Slovenia, Lithuania* and the *Czech Republic*, especially for under 3 year-olds). This is a particularly prohibitive problem in countries with a high proportion of private commercial ECEC centres such as the *United Kingdom*, especially in *England*.

11.7 Further challenges from a country expert perspective

- In 13 countries, the need for comprehensive quality assurance systems are highlighted (e.g. in *Croatia, Latvia, Russia*) as well as procedures for the monitoring of quality (e.g. in *Luxembourg*).

- The extreme differences in the quality of services for under 3 year-olds (e.g. in the *Czech Republic, France, Poland*) is also seen as a problem that requires a clear policy framework and strategy.
- The insufficient funding of ECEC-related research projects is viewed as a further challenge for system-related quality development (e.g. *Portugal, Spain*).
- A lack of differentiated national statistical data (especially with regard to under 3 year-olds in ECEC) is repeatedly cited as a problem for the research and evaluation of ECEC systems (e.g. in *Italy, Malta, Switzerland*).
- In several countries, a lack of knowledge among professionals in the areas of inclusion (e.g. in *Croatia*, the *Czech Republic*) and also information technologies and digitalisation (e.g. in *Sweden*) is seen as a challenge for the qualification systems and for which in some cases a revision of the early education curricula also seems appropriate.
- A lack of support measures for management and leadership (e.g. in *Sweden*) and insufficient professional networks (e.g. in *The Netherlands*) present challenges in some countries.
- Another problematic issue is the perceived lack of measures to reduce the proportion of unqualified staff (e.g. in *Austria, Denmark, Lithuania, Sweden*).
- Excessive bureaucratic requirements – especially for managers – are reported as a burden (e.g. in *Greece, Russia, Spain*) which negatively impacts on pedagogical practice by reducing the time available for reflection, planning or participation in professional development measures.

12 Summary and outlook

Each chapter in this book highlights a number of converging and diverging country-specific features relevant for understanding the ECEC workforce in the 33 countries represented in the SEEPRO-3 project. One thing that has become clear is that the systems of early childhood education and care in almost all countries are characterised by a certain dynamism – an indicator of this are the many reported initiatives and reforms concerning both the workforce and the overall system of early childhood education and care.

However, it is not only this dynamism that makes 'comparing' and searching for commonalities across countries a complex undertaking, but also the need to acknowledge the specific histories and traditions, the differing underpinning cultural beliefs and values and the diverse policy philosophies and strategies. This diversity defies overhasty judgements and hurried solutions. On the contrary, our understanding of 'comparing' has more in common with a 'science of difference' (Nóvoa 2018). Our analyses therefore primarily highlight differences between the countries, leaving readers to judge and draw conclusions based on their knowledge and experience of the workforce in their own ECEC system.

We start with a summary of the preceding chapters.

12.1 Contextual framework

The ECEC systems in the SEEPRO-3 countries can be categorised according to *three different system types* and five key criteria. In *unitary* systems (ten countries), there is *one* legal framework, *one* responsible ministry, *one* curriculum, *one* main type of setting and *one* core professional for all ECEC settings before primary schooling. A further ten countries are characterised by a *part-integrated* ECEC system in which early childhood education and care is the responsibility of *one* ministry, but the other four criteria are only partially fulfilled. More than a third of the countries (13) have a *bi-sectoral* system in which the responsibilities for 'childcare', on the one hand, and 'pre-primary education', on the other, are divided and more or less all corresponding criteria differ (an exception are the qualification requirements for core practitioners in *Portugal*, which are the same across both sectors).

Although almost all SEEPRO-3 countries provide a *legal entitlement* to a place in an ECEC centre for each child – at least from a certain age – a decision to introduce *compulsory enrolment* for a legally defined period has only been made in 21 countries.

The proportion of *public service providers* for ECEC centres for under 3 year-olds is generally not as high as for facilities for over 3 or 4 year-olds – especially in part-integrated and bi-sectoral ECEC systems, where *private providers* are more likely to be found. In countries with a unitary ECEC system, however, ECEC providers generally tend to be public.

In terms of *enrolment rates* (2022), the range is also extreme for the under-3 year-olds, from just over 2% to almost three quarters of the age group attending ECEC centres. In contrast, the range for over 3 year-olds is not as wide, with between just over 60% and 100% enrolled in an ECEC centre.

In all SEEPRO-3 countries, there is a mandatory *framework curriculum* for the age group from 3 or 4 years to school entry. However, guidelines for working with children under the age of 3 are only mandatory in the unitary ECEC systems and otherwise less regulated and rarely binding.

Evaluation measures as a criterion for quality development are analysed on a country-specific basis: child-related assessments, which are mostly carried out by core professionals, are the rule in two thirds of the SEEPRO-3 countries, but are rarely obligatory. In contrast, centre-based self-evaluation procedures are mandatory in 23 countries, particularly in centres for children over 3 or 4 years of age. The intervals between the mostly mandatory external evaluations of ECEC centres in settings for both age groups are usually three to five years.

All SEEPRO-3 countries are – albeit to varying degrees – on the way towards an *inclusive approach* to ECEC. In two thirds of the countries, children with disabilities and special educational needs are encouraged to attend mainstream facilities whenever possible. Prerequisites for the appropriate support of these children are specially qualified staff and sufficient funding for the centres.

Relevant *social and family policy aspects* are parental employment conditions and the issue of continuity between parenting leave and a guaranteed place in an ECEC setting. Although the proportion of working mothers has risen in most countries over the last decade, it is still significantly lower than that of fathers, particularly in certain countries. If the modalities of maternity and parental leave are not adequately designed to meet the needs of parents, there may be a (sometimes considerable) gap between the end of parental leave and an entitlement to a place in an ECEC centre. In most countries with a unitary or part-integrated ECEC system, it is generally possible to enrol a child in a centre directly after leave ends. In eight of the 13 countries with a bi-sectoral system, however, there are significant gaps between the end of parental leave and ECEC entitlement.

12.2 Early childhood staff

For *core professionals*, i.e. group-leading staff who work directly with children, a Bachelor's degree or comparable qualification is the minimum requirement in countries with a *unitary* ECEC system, as well as in seven of the ten countries with a *part-integrated* system. In countries with a *bi-sectoral* system, core practitioners who work with children under the age of 3 or 4 are differently qualified to those who work with older children. The latter are significantly more likely to have an education-related university degree. To take up the position of *centre leader*, a certain amount of professional experience is required, but in most cases no further qualification beyond the requirements for core pedagogues. In some cases, however, a specific management qualification is also required. Core professionals are sometimes supported in their day-to-day work by *assistant co-workers*, who generally have a significantly lower level of training and are more frequently deployed in the state education sectors than in the childcare sectors.

The majority of core professionals in the SEEPRO-3 countries work *full time*. In contrast, significant differences (from 1 to 18 hours per week) can be observed with regard to 'indirect' pedagogical working hours (*non-contact time*), which professionals can use for planning, preparation, team consultations, cooperation with parents or networking activities without direct contact with children.

In a number of countries, ECEC centres are supported by specialist *ECEC counsellors*, who can have both an advisory function and, in some cases, a supervisory function – or both. The professional profiles of these specialists vary greatly depending on the ECEC system, whether in the childcare or education sector and/or the qualification requirements. Beyond this, *specialist support staff*, such as Psychologists or Speech Therapists, with a primary focus on children with special educational needs, are deployed in diverse ways to support children (also staff and parents). In most SEEPRO-3 countries, external services are utilised for this purpose, while support provided by in-house specialists is available in some countries but not so common overall.

Specified personal and professional *competences* that prospective core practitioners should have vary considerably across the SEEPRO-3 countries and cannot be easily reduced to an overview. However, they can be divided into three main types, which are based on national legislation, defined by individual training institutions or defined by provider organisations in terms of commercial standards – especially in highly privatised childcare systems. The *curricula* for initial professional education courses in the SEEPRO-3 countries are similarly varied, some of which are drawn up nationally, others by individual universities and IPE institutions. With regard to the *field practice* part of initial professional education, there are more similarities across countries: as a rule, students begin by observing everyday practice in an ECEC setting and the activities of experienced professionals; they then go through a phase of planning, preparing and carrying out specific activities under supervision; and finally, a phase of independent work with children follows. Core competences include transferring theoretical knowledge into practice and reflecting on one's own role. However, the duration of the practicum or internship, the ECTS credits awarded (between 10 and 75 ECTS) and the availability of supervision by qualified mentors are handled very differently in the various countries.

Alternative training routes or *lateral entry measures* into the field are becoming increasingly important due to the severe shortage of staff in many countries. This means that – under certain conditions, which should not disregard the quality of professionalism – persons without the regular core practitioner IPE qualification can also help to support ECEC centre teams. In the majority of SEEPRO-3 countries, there are various routes into the profession: via special qualifying procedures, via additional training, and via the recognition of existing qualifications (sometimes acquired in another country) or (informal) competences.

Continuing professional development in the ECEC field is particularly effective if it is gauged towards the current qualification needs of staff and carried out on a regular, supervised and long-term basis. However, framework legislation and regulations, providers and main forms, obligation to attend and current thematic focuses differ considerably in the SEEPRO-3 countries. In most countries with bi-sectoral ECEC systems, CPD frameworks are more favourable for professionals working in the education sectors with over 3 or 4 year-olds than for practitioners in the childcare sectors.

Support for *newly qualified staff* through a regulated probationary and induction period is most common in the unitary systems and in the education sectors of the bi-sectoral ECEC systems and may also differ according to the ECEC provider. As a rule, new staff are accompanied by specially qualified mentors or by experienced staff members.

Overall, it has become clear how heterogeneous the workforce profiles in the 33 SEEPRO-3 countries are. Whether looking at the overall composition of the workforce in each country, the formal levels of initial professional education, the professional profiles of core practitioners or the provision of complementary ECEC specialists, it is the diversity that is particularly striking.

12.3 Reform strategies – staff and system-related challenges

A number of *nationwide reforms and policy initiatives* have not only aimed at strengthening the initial professional education of ECEC professionals but also at adapting it to changing contextual conditions (e.g. staff shortages). Welcome improvements regarding the working conditions of early childhood education and care staff have been taking place in some countries in terms of salary increases (albeit starting from a mostly low level) or other financial incentives and also a focus on career advancement. These measures are linked to the hope of counteracting staff shortages and retaining existing staff or attracting new interested persons to the profession. In two thirds of the SEEPRO-3 countries, staff shortages are cited as a particularly pressing problem and are mostly attributed to unfavourable working conditions or an ageing workforce.

Several countries have also adopted long-term national policy strategies aimed at the education system as a whole and which are also likely to have consequences for ECEC professionals. For example, individual countries emphasise the need, among other things, to strive for competent and motivated ECEC staff and leaders, or to improve conditions for career changers, as well as to create new positions in the ECEC centres for supporting newly qualified staff and students during their field practice.

Challenges reported from the perspective of country experts focus, on the one hand on ECEC staff and staffing issues and, on the other hand, to the ECEC system as a whole.

At the *staff-related* level, four challenges in particular are emphasised. Firstly, *staff shortages* and the lack of qualified professionals are frequently cited as the most prominent problem. Inadequate working conditions, low social prestige and low pay continue to be cited as the – by now well-known – reasons for this. A second problem area is the inadequate *staff to child ratio* in many cases and – due to the overall lack of staff – the increasing number of children in the group. Thirdly, in well over half of the countries, challenges are described with regard to the *initial professional education* of staff. In some the lack of regulations and specified qualification profiles for persons who wish to work with children under the age of 3 are criticised; in others, it is the need for better monitoring and more specific regulations for the sometimes very diverse university study programmes for prospective ECEC professionals. Finally, problematic aspects are raised with regard to the *continuing professional development* of core practitioners, leaders/managers and assistants, including the lack of substitute staff or the more advantageous access options for staff working in public ECEC centres compared with those employed in private settings.

At the *system level*, a *lack of coordination* between the childcare and education sectors is seen as a problem, particularly by the experts from countries with bi-sectoral ECEC systems. Even in countries that are already making their way towards a unitary system, financial challenges, clarification of professional profiles, functions and roles or the revision of curricula are seen as particularly pressing challenges. More than half of the country experts are critical of the lack of *equitable access* to high-quality ECEC *for all children*, heightened by a lack of available places or fees that are unaffordable for parents, and see this as a problem that needs to be addressed more effectively through targeted policy measures. Other reported problems include, for example, the *differences in the quality of provision* for under 3 year-olds and over 3 year-olds, a lack of specialist knowledge among professionals about inclusion and information technologies and digitalisation, as well as a lack of support measures for leaders and the sometimes excessive bureaucracy involved in managing ECEC centres.

12.4 Outlook

It can be assumed that the European systems of early childhood education and care will continue to be characterised by a marked dynamism. This is underpinned by the many reform initiatives that are underway or have been recently implemented in the countries. Therefore, this book publication and the online reports (https://www.seepro.eu) on ECEC workforce profiles and key contextual data cannot be seen as static reports: ECEC systems and also their policy environments are continuously on the move. The *Barcelona targets* revised by the European Commission in 2022 are also on the horizon. These are likely to have consequences for the further expansion of places in ECEC settings and increase the need for qualified specialists in an already strained staffing situation. The challenges faced by the ECEC systems in the SEEPRO-3 countries will therefore continue to exist. Not only does this mean that the staff already engaged and working to their limits need to be more highly valued in societal and material terms, but that ensuring a just system of early childhood education and care needs to be placed ever higher as a policy priority and to be seen clearly as a responsibility for society as a whole.

References

Ancheta-Arrabal, Ana (2024): *Spain* – ECEC Workforce Profile. In: Oberhuemer, Pamela/ Schreyer, Inge (Eds.): Early childhood workforce profiles across Europe. 33 country reports with key contextual data. Munich: State Institute for Early Childhood Research and Media Literacy. www.seepro.eu/Complete-Publication2024.pdf, pp. 1661-1705.

Araújo, Sara Barros (2024): *Portugal* – ECEC Workforce Profile. In: Oberhuemer, Pamela/Schreyer, Inge (Eds.): Early childhood workforce profiles across Europe. 33 country reports with key contextual data. Munich: State Institute for Early Childhood Research and Media Literacy. www.seepro.eu/Complete-Publication2024.pdf, pp. 1314-1346.

Bekendtgørelse om uddannelsen til professionsbachelor som pædagog 2017 [Executive Order on the Professional Bachelor's Degree Programme in Education]. BEK nr. 354 af 07/04/2017. København: Uddannelses- og Forskningsministeriet [Kopenhagen: Ministry of Education and Research]. https://www.retsinformation.dk/eli/lta/2017/354.

Binder, Julia (2024): 'Aufbewahrt statt erzogen': Brandbrief gegen Kita-Quereinsteiger ['Custodial care instead of education': Urgent letter against lateral entrants in ECEC centres]. https://www.br.de/nachrichten/bayern/aufbewahrt-statt-erzogen-brandbrief-gegen-kita-quereinsteiger,TupsBvw.

BMFSFJ – Bundesministerium für Familie, Senioren, Frauen und Jugend [Federal Ministry for Family Affairs, Senior Citizens, Women and Youth] (2024): Gesamtstrategie Fachkräfte in Kitas und Ganztag - Empfehlungen der AG Gesamtstrategie Fachkräfte [Overall strategy for professionals in ECEC and all-day provision – working group recommendations]. Berlin: BMFSFJ. https://www.bmfsfj.de/resource/blob/240068/eec13f657847909b2a024f9dffa1df02/gesamtstrategie-fachkraefte-in-kitas-und-ganztag-empfehlungen-der-ag-data.pdf.

Bouillet, Dejana (2024): *Croatia* – ECEC Workforce Profile. In: Oberhuemer, Pamela/ Schreyer, Inge (Eds.): Early childhood workforce profiles across Europe. 33 country reports with key contextual data. Munich: State Institute for Early Childhood Research and Media Literacy. www.seepro.eu/Complete-Publication2024.pdf, pp. 206-232.

Bulgarian government Directive for State Requirements for Attainment of the Professional Qualification of 'Teacher', dated 11.11.2016 and last updated on 05.02.2021. https://web.mon.bg/upload/25218/nrdb-kvalifikacia-uchitel_050221.pdf (in Bulgarian).

CARE – Curriculum Quality Analysis and Impact Review (2015): Comparative review of professional development approaches. https://ecec-care.org/fileadmin/careproject/Publications/reports/report_-_Comparative_review_of_professional_development_approaches.pdf.

Chydenius, Heidi (2024): *Finland* – ECEC Workforce Profile. In: Oberhuemer, Pamela/Schreyer, Inge (Eds.): Early childhood workforce profiles across Europe. 33 country reports with key contextual data. Munich: State Institute for Early Childhood Research and Media Literacy. www.seepro.eu/Complete-Publication2024.pdf, pp. 473-503.

Ciolan, Laura Elena/Petrescu, Anca/Bucur, Cristian/Colniceanu, Tania (2024): *Romania* – ECEC Workforce Profile. In: Oberhuemer, Pamela/Schreyer, Inge (Eds.): Early childhood workforce profiles across Europe. 33 country reports with key contextual data. Munich: State Institute for Early Childhood Research and Media Literacy. www.seepro.eu/Complete-Publication2024.pdf, pp. 1365-1397.

Council of the European Union (2019). Council Recommendation of 22 May 2019 on High-Quality Early Childhood Education and Care Systems. Official Journal of the European Union (No. OJ 2019/C189/03). https://eur-lex.europa.eu/legal-content/EN/TXT/PDF/?uri=CELEX:32019H0605(01)&rid=4.

Council of the European Union (2022): Council recommendation on early childhood education and care: The Barcelona targets for 2030. Brussels: Council of the European Union. https://eur-lex.europa.eu/legal-content/EN/TXT/PDF/?uri=CELEX:32022H1220(01)

Croatian Official Gazette – Narodne novine Nr. 30 (2021): Nacionalna razvojna strategija do 2030. godine [National Development Strategy 2030]. https://narodne-novine.nn.hr/clanci/sluzbeni/2021_02_13_230.html.

Dambrauskiene, Dalia/Liukineviciene, Laima (2018): The development of distributed leadership in Lithuanian early childhood education institutions. In: Socialiniai tyrimai, 41, 2, pp. 48-60. https://doi.org/10.21277/st.v41i2.252.

Danish Agency for Higher Education and Science – Uddannelses- og Forskningsstyrelsen. 2021. Evaluering af pædagoguddannelsen. Samlet rapport [Evaluation of the teacher education programme. Comprehensive report]. https://ufm.dk/publikationer/2021/evaluering-af-paedagoguddannelsen/hovedrapport.pdf.

Danish Ministerial Decree on the study programme for Bachelor in Social Education – Bekendtgørelse om uddannelsen til professionsbachelor som pædagog (2017): BEK nr. 354 af 07/04/2017. København: Uddannelses- og Forskningsministeriet. https://www.retsinformation.dk/eli/lta/2017/354.

DeGEval – Deutsche Gesellschaft für Evaluation e.V. (2016): Standards für Evaluation [Standards for evaluation]. https://www.uni-wuerzburg.de/fileadmin/ext00267/Dokumente/Evaluation/DeGEval-Standards_fuer_Evaluation_ersteRevision2016.pdf.

De Moll, Frederick/Kemp, Valérie/Simoes Loureiro, Kevin/Hadjar, Andreas/Kirsch, Claudine (2024): *Luxembourg* – ECEC Workforce Profile. In: Oberhuemer, Pamela/Schreyer, Inge (Eds.): Early childhood workforce profiles across Europe. 33 country reports with key contextual data. Munich: State Institute for Early Childhood Research and Media Literacy. www.seepro.eu/Complete-Publication2024.pdf, pp. 1021-1059.

Duignan, Maresa (2024): *Ireland* – ECEC Workforce Profile. In: Oberhuemer, Pamela/ Schreyer, Inge (Eds.): Early childhood workforce profiles across Europe. 33 country reports with key contextual data. Munich: State Institute for Early Childhood Research and Media Literacy. www.seepro.eu/Complete-Publication2024.pdf, pp. 811-842.

Dutch Education Professions Act (2013): Wet op de beroepen in het onderwijs. https://wetten.overheid.nl/BWBR0016944/2013-07-04.

Engels-Kritidis, Rozalina (2024): *Bulgaria* – ECEC Workforce Profile. In: Oberhuemer, Pamela/Schreyer, Inge (Eds.): Early childhood workforce profiles across Europe. 33 country reports with key contextual data. Munich: State Institute for Early Childhood Research and Media Literacy. www.seepro.eu/Complete-Publication2024.pdf, pp. 161–186.

Eurofound (2015): Early childhood care: working conditions, training and quality of services – A systematic review. Luxembourg: Publications Office of the European Union.

European Commission Network on Childcare and other measures to reconcile employment and family responsibilities (1996): Quality Targets in Services for Young Children. Proposals for a Ten Year Action Programme. Brussels: European Commission.

European Commission (2014): Proposal for Key Principles of a Quality Framework for Early Childhood Education and Care. Brussels: European Commission. Working Group on Early Childhood Education and Care under the auspices of the European Commission. https://www.opgroeien.be/sites/default/files/documenten/ecec-quality-framework_en.pdf.

European Commission, Directorate-General for Education, Youth, Sport and Culture (2018): Monitoring the Quality of Early Childhood Education and Care – Complementing the 2014 ECEC Quality Framework proposal with indicators. Recommendations from ECEC experts. Brussels: European Commission.

European Commission, Directorate-General for Education, Youth, Sport and Culture (2021): Early childhood education and care: how to recruit, train and motivate well-qualified staff. Final report. Publications Office of the European Union. https://data.europa.eu/doi/10.2766/489043.

European Commission (2022): A European Care Strategy for caregivers and care receivers. https://ec.europa.eu/commission/presscorner/detail/en/ip_22_5169.

European Commission/EACEA/Eurydice (2019a): Key Data on Early Childhood Education and Care in Europe – 2019 Edition. Eurydice Report. Luxembourg: Publications Office of the European Union. https://data.europa.eu/doi/10.2797/966808.

European Commission/EACEA/Eurydice (2019b): Eurydice Brief: Key Data on Early Childhood Education and Care in Europe. Luxembourg: Publications Office of the European Union. https://data.europa.eu/doi/10.2797/937677.

European Commission/EACEA/Eurydice (2023): Structural indicators for monitoring education and training systems in Europe 2023: early childhood education and

care. Publications Office of the European Union. https://data.europa.eu/doi/10.2797/670097.
European Commission Working Group on Early Childhood Education and Care (2023): Staff shortages in the early childhood education and care sector. Policy brief. Publications Office of the European Union.
Eurydice (2024): Poland: Special education needs provision within mainstream education, 12.1. https://eurydice.eacea.ec.europa.eu/national-education-systems/poland/special-education-needs-provision-within-mainstream-education.
[EVC] – Erkenning Verworven Competencie Branchestandaard (2021): Startbekwame pedagogisch medewerker kinderopvang [Entry-level qualified childcare worker]. https://www.kinderopvang-werkt.nl/werknemers/evc-procedure-startbekwame-pedagogisch-medewerker-kinderopvang.
Fielding, Michael/Moss, Peter (2011): Radical education and the common school: a democratic alternative. Abingdon: Routledge.
General Secretariat EDK Generalsekretariat EDK (2007): Kindergarten-Obligatorium, effektiver Besuch [Compulsory kindergarten, effective attendance]. https://www.edk.ch/de/bildungssystem/kantonale-schulorganisation/kantonsumfrage/a11-kindergarten-obligatorium.
Gulbrandsen, Lars (2024): *Norway* – ECEC Workforce Profile. In: Oberhuemer, Pamela/Schreyer, Inge (Eds.): Early childhood workforce profiles across Europe. 33 country reports with key contextual data. Munich: State Institute for Early Childhood Research and Media Literacy. www.seepro.eu/Complete-Publication2024.pdf, pp. 1227-1245.
[GUS] Główny Urząd Statystyczny – Statistics Poland (2023a): Education in the 2022/23 school year (pre-liminary data). https://stat.gov.pl/en/topics/education/education/education-in-the-school-year- 20222023-preliminary-data,13,1.html.
[GUS] Główny Urząd Statystyczny – Statistics Poland (2023b): Nurseries and kids' clubs in 2022. https://stat.gov.pl/en/topics/children-and-family/children/nurseries-and-childrens-clubs-in- 2022,2,10.html.
Heikka, Johanna/Hujala, Eeva (2013): Early childhood leadership through the lens of distributed leadership. In: European Early Childhood Education Research Journal 21, 4, pp. 568-580, https://doi.org/10.1080/1350293X.2013.845444.
Hostettler Schärer, Janine (2024): *Switzerland* – ECEC Workforce Profile. In: Oberhuemer, Pamela/Schreyer, Inge (Eds.): Early childhood workforce profiles across Europe. 33 country reports with key contextual data. Munich: State Institute for Early Childhood Research and Media Literacy. www.seepro.eu/Complete-Publication2024.pdf, pp. 1776-1807.
International Network on Leave Policies & Research (2023a): Cross-country comparisons – leave and ECEC entitlements. https://www.leavenetwork.org/fileadmin/user_upload/k_leavenetwork/annual_reviews/2023/3.5._Leave_ECEC_Entitlements.pdf.
International Network on Leave Policies & Research (2023b): Country reports. https://www.leavenetwork.org/annual-review-reports/country-reports/.

[ISTAT] Italian National Institute of Statistics (2023): Schools: Pre-primary-schools, classes, children. http://dati.istat.it/Index.aspx?QueryId=36871&lang=en.

Jager, Jerneja (2024): *Slovenia* – ECEC Workforce Profile. In: Oberhuemer, Pamela/Schreyer, Inge (Eds.): Early childhood workforce profiles across Europe. 33 country reports with key contextual data. Munich: State Institute for Early Childhood Research and Media Literacy. www.seepro.eu/Complete-Publication2024.pdf, pp. 1598-1638.

Jensen, Bente/Iannone, Rosa Lisa (2018): Innovative approaches to continuous professional development (CPD) in early childhood education and care (ECEC) in Europe: Findings from a comparative review. In: European Journal of Education, Research, Development and Policy, 53, 1, pp. 23-33.

Jensen, Charlotte Riis/Preus, Marianne (2020): Faglige fyrtårne – et voksende fænomen på dagtilbudsområdet [Professional beacons – a growing phenomenon in the ECEC field]. In: FPPU. 4, 2, pp. 80-93. https://tidsskrift.dk/FPPU/article/view/122505/169684.

Kagan, Sharon Lynn/Roth, Jessica L. (2017): Transforming Early Childhood Systems for Future Generations: Obligations and Opportunities. In: International Journal of Early Childhood 49, pp. 137–154. DOI 10.1007/s13158-017-0194-4.

Kaiser, Anna-Katharina/Fuchs-Rechlin, Kirsten (2020): Steuerung der Qualität oder Qualität der Steuerung? Die gesetzliche Rahmung der Kita-Fachberatung in den Bundesländern [Control of quality or quality of control? The legal framework of ECEC counsellors and supervisors in the federal states]. https://www.weiterbildungsinitiative.de/fileadmin/Redaktion/Publikationen/WiFF_Arbeitspapier_3_Fachberatung.pdf.

Karlsson Lohmander, Maelis (2024): *Sweden* – ECEC Workforce Profile. In: Oberhuemer, Pamela/Schreyer, Inge (Eds.): Early childhood workforce profiles across Europe. 33 country reports with key contextual data. Munich: State Institute for Early Childhood Research and Media Literacy. www.seepro.eu/Complete-Publication2024.pdf, pp. 1724-1754.

Klinkhammer, Nicole/Schäfer, Britta/Harring, Dana/Gwinner, Anne (2017): Qualitätsmonitoring in der frühkindlichen Bildung und Betreuung. Ansätze und Erfahrungen aus ausgewählten Ländern [Quality monitoring in early childhood education and care. Approaches and experiences from selected countries]. Munich: Verlag Deutsches Jugendinstitut.

[KMK] Sekretariat der ständigen Konferenz der Kultusminister der Länder in der Bundesrepublik Deutschland (2017): Kompetenzorientiertes Qualifikationsprofil für die Ausbildung von Erzieherinnen und Erziehern an Fachschulen und Fachakademien [Competence-oriented qualification profile for prospective Educators at vocational technical colleges/academies. Resolution adopted at the Standing Conference of Education Ministers on 01.12.2011, as amended on 24.11.2017]. http://www.kmk.org/fileadmin/Dateien/veroeffentlichungen_beschluesse/2011/2011_12_01-Er-zieherInnen-QualiProfil.pdf.

[KMK] Sekretariat der ständigen Konferenz der Kultusminister der Länder in der Bundesrepublik Deutschland (2020): Rahmenlehrplan für die Fachschule für Sozialpädagogik [Framework curriculum for vocational technical colleges specialising in social pedagogy. Resolution of the Standing Conference of the Ministers of Education and Cultural Affairs on 18.06.2020]. https://www.kmk.org/fileadmin/Dateien/veroeffentlichungen_beschluesse/2020/2020_06_18-RVFS-RLP-Sozpaed.pdf.

Koch, Anette Boye/Jensen, Jytte Juul (2024): *Denmark* – ECEC Workforce Profile. In: Oberhuemer, Pamela/Schreyer, Inge (Eds.): Early childhood workforce profiles across Europe. 33 country reports with key contextual data. Munich: State Institute for Early Childhood Research and Media Literacy. www.seepro.eu/Complete-Publication2024.pdf, 382-412.

Korintus, Marta (2024): *Hungary* – ECEC Workforce Profile. In: Oberhuemer, Pamela/Schreyer, Inge (Eds.): Early childhood workforce profiles across Europe. 33 country reports with key contextual data. Munich: State Institute for Early Childhood Research and Media Literacy. www.seepro.eu/Complete-Publication2024.pdf, pp. 765-790.

Krenn-Wache, Marisa (2024): *Austria* – ECEC Workforce Profile. In: Oberhuemer, Pamela/Schreyer, Inge (Eds.): Early childhood workforce profiles across Europe. 33 country reports with key contextual data. Munich: State Institute for Early Childhood Research and Media Literacy. www.seepro.eu/Complete-Publication2024.pdf, pp. 8–42.

Larsen, Trine P./de la Porte, Caroline (2022): Early Childhood Education and Care in Denmark: A Social Investment Success. In: De la Porte, Caroline/Eydal, Guðný Björk/Kauko, Jaakko/Nohrstedt, Daniel/'t Hart, Paul/Tranøy Bent Sofus (Eds.): Successful Public Policy in the Nordic Countries: Cases, Lessons, Challenges, pp. 66–87. Oxford: Oxford University Press. https://doi.org/10.1093/oso/9780192856296.003.0004.

Loizou, Eleni (2024): *Cyprus* – ECEC Workforce Profile. In: Oberhuemer, Pamela/Schreyer, Inge (Eds.): Early childhood workforce profiles across Europe. 33 country reports with key contextual data. Munich: State Institute for Early Childhood Research and Media Literacy. www.seepro.eu/Complete-Publication2024.pdf, pp. 253-285.

Loudová Stralczynská, Barbora (2024): *Czech Republic* – ECEC Workforce Profile. In: Oberhuemer, Pamela/Schreyer, Inge (Eds.): Early childhood workforce profiles across Europe. 33 country reports with key contextual data. Munich: State Institute for Early Childhood Research and Media Literacy. www.seepro.eu/Complete-Publication2024.pdf, pp. 302-358.

Lumsden, Eunice, with Burton, Sarah/MacDonald, Natalie/Rogers, Catriona (2024): *United Kingdom* – ECEC Workforce Profile. In: Oberhuemer, Pamela/Schreyer, Inge (Eds.): Early childhood workforce profiles across Europe. 33 country reports with key contextual data. Munich: State Institute for Early Childhood Research

and Media Literacy. https://www.seepro.eu/Complete-Publication2024.pdf, pp. 1876-1956.
Lunneblad, Johannes/Garvis, Susanne (2017): A study of Swedish preschool directors' perspectives on leadership and organization. In: Early Child Development and Care 189, 6, pp. 938-945. https://doi.org/10.1080/03004430.2017.1354855.
Matković, Teo/Ostojić, Jelena/Lucić, Marko/Jaklin, Katarina/Ivšić, Iva 2020. Raditi u dječjim vrtićima: rezultati istraživanja uvjeta rada u ranom i predškolskom odgoju i obrazovanju [Working in kindergartens: research results on working conditions in ECEC]. Zagreb: Sindikat obrazovanja, medija i kulture Hrvatske & Baza za radničku inicijativu i demokraciju [Croatian Union of Education, Media and Culture & Base for Workers' Initiative and Democracy]. https://docplayer.rs/208286040-Raditi-u-dječjim-vrtićima-rezultati-istraživanja-uvjeta-rada-u-ranom-i-predškolskom-odgoju-i-obrazovanju.html.
Miňová, Monika/Lynch, Zuzana/Lipnická, Milena (2024): *Slovak Republic* – ECEC Workforce Profile. In: Oberhuemer, Pamela/Schreyer, Inge (Eds.): Early childhood workforce profiles across Europe. 33 country reports with key contextual data. Munich: State Institute for Early Childhood Research and Media Literacy. www.seepro.eu/Complete-Publication2024.pdf, pp. 1544-1576.
Miskeljin, Lidija (2024): *Serbia* – ECEC Workforce Profile. In: Oberhuemer, Pamela/Schreyer, Inge (Eds.): Early childhood workforce profiles across Europe. 33 country reports with key contextual data. Munich: State Institute for Early Childhood Research and Media Literacy. www.seepro.eu/Complete-Publication2024.pdf, pp. 1482-1523.
Moss, Peter/Mitchell, Linda (2024): Early Childhood in the Anglosphere. Systemic failings and transformative possibilities. London: UCL Press. https://doi.org/10.14324/111.9781800082533.
Nicholson, Julie/Maniates, Helen (2016): Recognizing Postmodern Intersectional Identities in Leadership for Early Childhood. In: Early Years: An International Journal of Research and Development, 36, pp. 66-80. https://doi.org/10.1080/09575146.2015.1080667.
Nicholson, Julie/Kuhl, Katie/Maniates, Helen/Lin, Betty/Bonetti, Sara (2020): A review of the literature on leadership in early childhood: Examining epistemological foundations and considerations of social justice. In: Early Child Development and Care 190, 2, pp. 91-122. https://doi.org/10.1080/03004430.2018.1455036.
Norwegian Ministry of Education and Research (2012): Forskrift om rammeplan for barnehagelærerutdanning [Regulations on the framework plan for Kindergarten Teacher training – in Norwegian]. https://www.regjeringen.no/no/dokumenter/rundskriv-f-04-12/id706946/?id=706946.
Nóvoa, Antonio (2018): Comparing Southern Europe: The Difference, the Public, and the Common.' In: Comparative Education 54, 4, pp. 548–561.

Oberhuemer, Pamela (2015): Seeking new cultures of cooperation: A cross-national analysis of workplace-based learning and mentoring practices in early years professional education/training. In: Early Years - an international research journal, 35, 2, pp. 115-123.

Oberhuemer, Pamela/Schreyer, Inge (Eds.) (2018): Early childhood workforce profiles in 30 countries with key contextual data. Munich. https://www.seepro.eu/ISBN-publication.pdf.

Oberhuemer, Pamela/Schreyer, Inge (2024a): *Germany* – ECEC Workforce Profile. In: Oberhuemer, Pamela/Schreyer, Inge (Eds.): Early childhood workforce profiles across Europe. 33 country reports with key contextual data. Munich: State Institute for Early Childhood Research and Media Literacy. www.seepro.eu/Complete-Publication2024.pdf, pp. 614-669.

Oberhuemer, Pamela/Schreyer (Eds.) (2024b): Early childhood workforce profiles across Europe. 33 country reports with key contextual data. Munich: State Institute for Early Childhood Research and Media Literacy. www.seepro.eu/Complete-Publication2024.pdf.

Oberhuemer, Pamela/Schreyer, Inge/Neuman, Michelle J. (2010): Professionals in Early Education and Care Systems – European Profiles and Perspectives. Opladen and Farmington Hills, MI: Barbara Budrich.

Oberhuemer, Pamela/Ulich, Michaela (1997): Working with young children in Europe. London: Paul Chapman Publishing Ltd.

OECD – Organisation for Economic Co-operation and Development (2001): Starting Strong: Early childhood education and care. Paris: OECD. Online. https://read.oecd-ilibrary.org/education/starting-strong_9789264192829-en#page3.

OECD – Organisation for Economic Co-operation and Development (2006): Starting Strong II: Early childhood education and care. Paris: OECD. Online. https://www.oecd.org/education/school/startingstrongiiearlychildhoodeducationandcare.htm (Note: The Starting Strong II review has been removed from the OECD website.)

OECD – Organisation for Economic Co-operation and Development (2015): Starting Strong IV. Monitoring Quality in Early Childhood Education and Care. https://www.oecd.org/education/starting-strong-iv-9789264268289-de.htm.

OECD – Organisation for Economic Co-operation and Development (2020): Curriculum (re)design. https://www.oecd.org/education/2030-project/contact/brochure-thematic-reports-on-curriculum-redesign.pdf.

Picchio, Mariacristina/Bove, Chiara (2024): *Italy* – ECEC Workforce Profile. In: Oberhuemer, Pamela/Schreyer, Inge (Eds.): Early childhood workforce profiles across Europe. 33 country reports with key contextual data. Munich: State Institute for Early Childhood Research and Media Literacy. www.seepro.eu/Complete-Publication2024.pdf, pp. 867-914.

Pirard, Florence/Peleman, Brecht/Sharmahd, Nima/van Laere, Katrin/Reinertz, Catherine/Backes, Jana (2024): *Belgium* – ECEC Workforce Profile. In: Oberhuemer, Pamela/Schreyer, Inge (Eds.): Early childhood workforce profiles across Europe. 33 country reports with key contextual data. Munich: State Institute for Early

Childhood Research and Media Literacy. www.seepro.eu/Complete-Publication2024.pdf, pp. 64–130

Portuguese decree law no. 79 (2014): Aprova o regime jurídico da habilitação profissional para a docência na educação pré-escolar e nos ensinos básico e secundário [Approves the legal regime for professional qualifications for teaching in pre-school, basic and secondary education]. (D.R. n. 92, Série I, 14 May 2014: 2819-2828). https://dre.pt/dre/detalhe/decreto-lei/79-2014-25344769

Rayna, Sylvie (2024): *France* – ECEC Workforce Profile. In: Oberhuemer, Pamela/Schreyer, Inge (Eds.): Early childhood workforce profiles across Europe. 33 country reports with key contextual data. Munich: State Institute for Early Childhood Research and Media Literacy. www.seepro.eu/Complete-Publication2024.pdf, pp. 523-590.

Sabaliauskas, Eigirsdas/Siarova, Hanna (2024): *Lithuania* – ECEC Workforce Profile. In: Oberhuemer, Pamela/Schreyer, Inge (Eds.): Early childhood workforce profiles across Europe. 33 country reports with key contextual data. Munich: State Institute for Early Childhood Research and Media Literacy. www.seepro.eu/Complete-Publication2024.pdf, pp. 975-1001.

Sakellariou, Maria (2024): *Greece* – ECEC Workforce Profile. In: Oberhuemer, Pamela/Schreyer, Inge (Eds.): Early childhood workforce profiles across Europe. 33 country reports with key contextual data. Munich: State Institute for Early Childhood Research and Media Literacy. www.seepro.eu/Complete-Publication2024.pdf, pp. 700-745.

Sakr, Mona/O'Sullivan, June (2022): Dialogical conceptualisations of leadership in social enterprise early years. In: Early Years – an international research journal 43, 4-5, pp. 938-951. https://doi.org/10.1080/09575146.2022.2036950.

Sharmahd Nima/Peeters, Jan/Van Laere, Katrien/Vonta, Tatjana/De Kimpe, Chris/Brajković, Sanja/Contini, Laura/Giovannini, Donatella (2017): Transforming European ECEC services and primary schools into profes-sional learning communities: drivers, barriers and ways forward, NESET II report, Luxembourg: Publications Office of the European Union. doi: 10.2766/74332.

Singer, Elly/Romijn, Bodine (2024): *The Netherlands* – ECEC Workforce Profile. In: Oberhuemer, Pamela/Schreyer, Inge (Eds.): Early childhood workforce profiles across Europe. 33 country reports with key contextual data. Munich: State Institute for Early Childhood Research and Media Literacy. www.seepro.eu/Complete-Publication2024.pdf, pp. 1176-1207.

Sofii, Nataliia (2024): *Ukraine* – ECEC Workforce Profile. In: Oberhuemer, Pamela/Schreyer, Inge (Eds.): Early childhood workforce profiles across Europe. 33 country reports with key contextual data. Munich: State Institute for Early Childhood Research and Media Literacy. www.seepro.eu/Complete-Publication2024.pdf, pp. 1829-1855.

Sollars, Valerie (2024): *Malta* – ECEC Workforce Profile. In: Oberhuemer, Pamela/Schreyer, Inge (Eds.): Early childhood workforce profiles across Europe. 33 country reports with key contextual data. Munich: State Institute for Early Childhood

Research and Media Literacy. www.seepro.eu/Complete-Publication2024.pdf, pp. 1087-1154.

Sousa, Diana/Moss, Peter (2022): Concluding reflections: current issues and future directions for comparative studies in early childhood education. In: Comparative Education, 58(3), pp. 402–416. https://doi.org/10.1080/03050068.2022.2071018.

Spanish Ministry of Education and Vocational Training – Ministerio de educación y formación professional (2023): Datos y cifras curso escolar 2023/2024 [Facts and figures for the school year 2023/24]. https://www.educacionyfp.gob.es/dam/jcr:27162db1-c2b3-4f9c-a8fa-a17731a561f8/datos-y-cifras-2023-2024-espanol.pdf.

Spring, Heidi Honig/Spring, Frank (2020): Faglige fyrtårne og andre ressourcepersoner i dagtilbud. Viden og værktøjer [Professional beacons and other resource persons in ECEC. Knowledge and tools]. Dafolo. https://www.ucviden.dk/en/publications/faglige-fyrt%C3%A5rne-og-andre-ressourcepersoner-i-dagtilbud-viden-og-.

Statistics Norway (2023): Children allocated extra resources, by region, contents and year. https://www.ssb.no/en/statbank/table/12376/tableViewLayout1/.

Šūpule, Inese (2024): *Latvia* – ECEC Workforce Profile. In: Oberhuemer, Pamela/Schreyer, Inge (Eds.): Early childhood workforce profiles across Europe. 33 country reports with key contextual data. Munich: State Institute for Early Childhood Research and Media Literacy. www.seepro.eu/Complete-Publication2024.pdf, pp. 934-958.

Swiss Federal Statistical Office – Bundesamt für Statistik. 2023. Obligatorische Schule, Sekundarstufe II, Tertiärstufe - höhere Fachschulen [Compulsory school, upper secondary level, tertiary level - higher vocational colleges]. https://www.bfs.admin.ch/bfs/de/home/statistiken/bildung-wissenschaft/personal-bildungsinstitutionen/obligatorische-schule-sekundarstufe-II-tertiaerstufe-hoehere-fachschulen.html.

Ukrainian Ministry of Economics (2021): *Order 'On Approval of the Professional Standard Early Childhood Teacher'* (19.10.2021) [in Ukrainian]. https://mon.gov.ua/ua/npa/pro-zatverdzhennya-profesijnogo-standartu-vihovatel-zakladu-doshkilnoyi-osviti.

UNESCO Institute for Statistics (2012): International Standard Classification for Education – ISCED 2011. https://uis.unesco.org/sites/default/files/documents/international-standard-classification-of-education-isced-2011-en.pdf.

United Nations (1989): Convention on the Rights of the Child. https://www.ohchr.org/en/instruments-mechanisms/instruments/convention-rights-child.

United Nations (2006): Convention on the Rights of Persons with Disabilities. https://www.un.org/disabilities/documents/convention/convention_accessible_pdf.pdf.

University of Ljubljana, Faculty of Education (2023): Podatki študijskega programa Predšolska vzgoja [Data of the Pre-school Education Study Programme]. https://www.pef.uni-lj.si/wp-content/up-loads/2023/01/Predsolska-vzgoja.pdf.

Urban, Mathias/Vandenbroeck, Michel/Peeters, Jan/Lazzari, Arianna/Van der Laere, Katrien (2011): CoRe – Competence requirements in early childhood education and care. Final report. London/Ghent: University of East London/University of

Ghent. https://op.europa.eu/en/publication-detail/-/publication/fc7e05f4-30b9-480a-82a7-8afd99b7a723.

Veisson, Marika/Peterson, Tiina (2024): *Estonia* – ECEC Workforce Profile. In: Oberhuemer, Pamela/Schreyer, Inge (Eds.): Early childhood workforce profiles across Europe. 33 country reports with key contextual data. Munich: State Institute for Early Childhood Research and Media Literacy. www.seepro.eu/Complete-Publication2024.pdf, pp. 431-455.

Volkova, Tatiana (2024): *Russian Federation* – ECEC Workforce Profile. In: Oberhuemer, Pamela/Schreyer, Inge (Eds.): Early childhood workforce profiles across Europe. 33 country reports with key contextual data. Munich: State Institute for Early Childhood Research and Media Literacy. www.seepro.eu/Complete-Publication2024.pdf, pp. 1415-1453.

Weßler-Poßberg, Dagmar/Huschik, Gwendolyn/Hoch, Markus/Friederich, Tina (2022): Karrierewege in der Kindertagesbetreuung [Career paths in childcare]. https://www.bmfsfj.de/resource/blob/198224/c27a048ee0e68cce51bfa953dd6fd031/karrierewege-in-der-kindertagesbetreuung-prognos-studie-data.pdf.

Willekens, Harry/Scheiwe, Kirsten (2020): Looking back. Kindergarten and pre-school in Europe since the late 18th century. Hildesheim: Universitätsverlag. https://dx.doi.org/10.18442/126.

Williams, Pia/Sheridan, Sonja/Garvis, Susanne/Mellgren, Elisabeth (2018): Early childhood education and care in Sweden. In: Garvis, Susanne/Phillipson, Sivanes/Harju-Luukkainen, Heidi (Eds.) International perspectives on early childhood education and care, pp. 143-153. London, New York: Routledge.

Żytko, Małgorzata/Pacholczyk-Sanfilippo, Marta/Wysłowska, Olga (2024): *Poland* – ECEC Workforce Profile. In: Oberhuemer, Pamela/Schreyer, Inge (Eds.): Early childhood workforce profiles across Europe. 33 country reports with key contextual data. Munich: State Institute for Early Childhood Research and Media Literacy. www.seepro.eu/Complete-Publication2024.pdf, pp. 1264-1291.

About the authors

Pamela Oberhuemer is currently an Honorary Senior Research Fellow at the Thomas Coram Research Unit, IOE Faculty of Education and Society, University College London. In the mid-1970s she moved from London to Munich, where she was employed as a full-time researcher at the State Institute for Early Childhood Research and Media Literacy (IFP) for over 30 years. Since the mid-1990s her main research focus has been on systems of early childhood education and care in the European context, particularly on the early childhood workforce. In recent years she has worked as a freelance researcher and consultant for the IFP and the German Youth Institute (DJI). Together with Inge Schreyer, she completed the SEEPRO-3 study (2021-2024) on ECEC Workforce Profiles in Europe with funding from the German Federal Ministry for Family Affairs, Senior Citizens, Women and Youth. This was the fourth in a series of projects based at the IFP spanning multiple countries over a period of 30 years in which she played a leading role.

Inge Schreyer studied psychology at the Ludwig Maximilian University in Munich and completed her doctoral degree at the University of Regensburg in the field of educational psychology. Since 2000, she has been a senior researcher at the State Institute for Early Childhood Research and Media Literacy (IFP) in Munich. Her main focus has been on research and evaluation studies on the quality of ECEC provider services and on working conditions in ECEC settings. She contributed to the first SEEPRO study *Systems of Early Childhood Education and Professionalisation in Europe* (project leader: Pamela Oberhuemer), funded by the German Federal Ministry for Family and Youth Affairs and published in 2010 in English and German, and took over the management of the two follow-up studies with project starts in 2015 and 2021.

SEEPRO-3 Cooperation partners in 33 countries (2021–2024)

Austria	Marisa Krenn-Wache, formerly: BAfEP, Federal Vocational College for Early Childhood Pedagogy, Klagenfurt
Belgium	Florence Pirard, University of Liège
	Brecht Peleman, Nima Sharmahd, Katrien van Laere, VBJK– Centre for Innovation in the Early Years, Ghent
	Catherine Reinertz, Jana Backes, Ministry of the German-speaking Community, Eupen
Bulgaria	Rozalina Engels-Kritidis, University St. Kliment Ohridski, Sofia
Croatia	Dejana Bouillet, University of Zagreb
Cyprus	Eleni Loizou, University of Cyprus
Czech Republic	Barbora Loudová Stralczynská, Charles University, Prague
Denmark	Anette Boye Koch, Jytte Juul Jensen, VIA University College Aarhus
Estonia	Marika Veisson, University of Tallinn
	Tiina Peterson, Estonian Ministry of Education and Research (from August 2024: University of Tartu)
Finland	Heidi Chydenius, University of Helsinki
France	Sylvie Rayna, EXPÉRICE, University Sorbonne Paris Nord
Germany	Pamela Oberhuemer, University College London, TCRU; formerly: State Institute for Early Childhood Research and Media Literacy (IFP), Munich
	Inge Schreyer, State Institute for Early Childhood Research and Media Literacy (IFP), Munich
	Assessments of current challenges:
	Sigrid Ebert, formerly: Pestalozzi-Fröbel-Haus, Berlin
	Sigrid Lorenz, State Institute for Early Childhood Research and Media Literacy (IFP), Munich
Greece	Maria Sakellariou, University of Ioannina
Hungary	Marta Korintus, formerly: Institute for Family, Youth and Population Policy, Budapest
Ireland	Maresa Duignan, Department of Education, Dublin
Italy	Mariacristina Picchio, National Research Council, Rome
	Chiara Bove, University of Milan-Bicocca
Latvia	Inese Šūpule, Baltic Institute of Social Sciences, Riga
Lithuania	Hanna Siarova, Eigirdas Sabaliauskas, Radvile Bankauskaite, Public Policy and Management Institute, Vilnius

Luxembourg	Claudine Kirsch, University of Luxembourg
	Frederick de Moll, University of Bielefeld, Germany
	Valérie Kemp, Kevin Simoes Loureiro, University of Luxembourg
	Andreas Hadjar, University of Fribourg, Switzerland
Malta	Valerie Sollars, University of Malta
The Netherlands	Bodine Romijn, University of Utrecht
	Elly Singer†, formerly: Universities of Utrecht and Amsterdam
Norway	Lars Gulbrandsen, Institute for Norwegian Social Research, Oslo Metropolitan University
Poland	Małgorzata Żytko, Marta Pacholczyk-Sanfilippo, Olga Wysłowska, University of Warsaw
Portugal	Sara Barros Araújo, Polytechnic University of Porto
Romania	Laura Elena Ciolan, Anca Petrescu, Cristian Bucur, Tania Colniceanu, University of Bucharest
Russian Federation	Tatiana Volkova, WFS Bildungs gUG, Berlin
Serbia	Lidija Miskeljin, University of Belgrade
Slovak Republic	Monika Miňová, University of Presov
	Zuzana Lynch, Milena Lipnicka, Matej Bel University Banská Bystrica
Slovenia	Jerneja Jager, Educational Research Institute, Step by Step Centre for Quality in Education, Ljubljana
Spain	Ana Ancheta-Arrabal, University of Valencia
Sweden	Maelis Karlsson Lohmander, University of Gothenburg
Switzerland	Janine Hostettler Schärer, St. Gallen University of Teacher Education
Ukraine	Nataliia Sofii, Ukrainian Institute of Education Development, Kyiv
United Kingdom	Eunice Lumsden, University of Northampton
	Contributing nation-specific specialists:
	Sarah Burton, Open University, Scotland
	Natalie MacDonald, University of Wales Trinity St. David
	Catriona Rogers, Stranmillis University College, Northern Ireland

Glossary

Age range format

International data sources use varying ways of presenting the age range of children enrolled in ECEC settings. We have chosen the following format for the SEEPRO-3 reports and this book: **0–2** for children up to 3 years of age and **3–5** for 3, 4 and 5 year-olds in countries with a primary school entry age of 6 years. Depending on the specific setting features in each country, these may appear as **0–3** (under 4 year-olds), **0–5** (under 6 year-olds), **4–5** (4 and 5 year-olds), and so on.

ECEC system types as categorised in this book

Unitary ECEC system

Five key criteria indicate a unitary early childhood education and care system for children of all ages up to the start of primary schooling:

- *One* national ministry/jurisdiction responsible for regulating all settings
- *One* legal framework for all ECEC settings from age 1 or under up to the start of primary schooling
- *One* curricular framework applying to all settings
- *One* main type of multi-age provision
- *One* type of core practitioner working with children across the ECEC phase.

Part-integrated ECEC system

One national ministry/jurisdiction with overall responsibility for governance but the other four criteria are not fully met. Federal or devolved systems are special cases, where meeting each of the criteria may vary.

Bi-sectoral ECEC system

- *Two* separate ministries/jurisdictions (occasionally three) responsible for different age groups or different types of ECEC setting
- *Separate* legal frameworks
- *Separate* curricular frameworks (sometimes none for children up to age 3)
- *Different* types of provision for different age groups.

– *Differently qualified* core practitioners working with children up to age 3 or 4 and above age 3 or 4

ECTS – European Credit Transfer and Accumulation System

A system for enhancing student mobility through the Europe-wide recognition of credit transfers and credit accumulation in higher education
https://education.ec.europa.eu/education-levels/higher-education/inclusive-and-connected-higher-education/european-credit-transfer-and-accumulation-system

EQF – European Qualifications Framework

Outcomes based (knowledge, skills, competences), eight-level reference tool to enable qualification comparisons between countries.
https://europass.europa.eu/en/europass-digital-tools/european-qualifications-framework

ISCED – International Standard Classification of Education

An instrument for comparing levels and fields of education across countries, developed by UNESCO in the 1970s and revised in 1997 and 2011.
https://uis.unesco.org/en/topic/international-standard-classification-education-isced

ISCED 2011 is used throughout this book to indicate the formal qualification levels of core practitioners and assistant co-workers, which are summarised below.

ISCED level 0 – Early childhood education
ISCED level 1 – Primary education
ISCED level 2 – Lower secondary education (general/vocational)
ISCED level 3 – Upper secondary education (general/vocational)
ISCED level 4 – Post-secondary non-tertiary education (general/vocational)
ISCED level 5 – Short-cycle tertiary education (general/vocational)
ISCED level 6 – Bachelor's or equivalent level (academic/professional)
ISCED level 7 – Master's or equivalent level (academic/professional)
ISCED level 8 – Doctoral or equivalent level (academic/professional)

Index

A
access to early childhood education and care 23ff, 126, 133
Ancheta-Arrabal, Ana 70, 82, 122, 150
Araújo, Sara Barros 82, 98f, 150
assistant co-workers 12, 73–75, 114, 123, 125, 131, 152
Austria 5, 11, 20f, 29, 33, 37f, 40f, 43ff, 47f, 50, 52, 55, 60f, 64ff, 74, 76f, 79, 81, 83, 93, 95f, 100, 107, 109, 111, 115, 119, 126f, 140, 149

B
Backes, Jana 149
Barcelona targets 41, 134
Belgium 5, 11, 21f, 25, 31, 35–39, 44, 47–52, 55, 62–67, 75, 78f, 82, 84, 100, 106f, 112, 114, 116, 120, 125, 149
Binder, Julia 105
bi-sectoral ECEC system 22, 25, 27, 35, 39ff, 44, 46, 59, 63, 75, 79, 82ff, 90, 92, 97, 101, 110f, 115, 130, 132f, 151
Bouillet, Dejana 81, 88, 111f, 121, 149
Bove, Chiara 78, 103, 122, 126, 149
Bucur, Cristian 150
Bulgaria 5, 11, 21f, 25, 28, 32, 35–38, 44, 46–50, 52ff, 63–66, 75, 78f, 93, 97–101, 116, 123, 125f, 149
Burton, Sarah 150

C
centre leaders 5, 8f, 13, 47f, 52, 59, 67–70, 72, 77, 103, 106, 112f, 115, 119f, 125, 131

Chydenius, Heidi 32, 93f, 149
Ciolan, Laura 150
Colniceanu, Tania 150
competences 85, 87–92, 96, 102, 105f, 131f, 152
compulsory enrolment 32–39, 129
continuing professional development (CPD) 13, 51f, 74, 77, 79, 105, 109–116, 120, 125, 132f
core practitioners 13, 59ff, 63ff, 66ff, 73f, 80f, 85–89, 92f, 100, 106, 109, 111, 114, 119f, 124f, 129, 131ff, 151
crèche/s 24, 28, 40f, 78
Croatia 5, 12, 19, 24, 29, 32, 37f, 40ff, 47ff, 52, 54f, 59f, 64–67, 73f, 76, 81, 83, 86, 88, 100f, 103, 105, 109f, 112, 114f, 121, 124–127, 149
curricular frameworks 26ff, 42–46, 52
Cyprus 5, 12, 21f, 25, 35, 37ff, 41, 44, 46, 49f, 52f, 55, 59, 63, 65f, 75, 78f, 82, 100, 116, 123, 149
Czech Republic 5, 11, 21, 25, 28f, 37f, 41, 44, 47f, 51, 53ff, 60, 64–67, 69, 75, 78f, 82f, 100, 106, 112ff, 116, 120f, 123f, 126f, 149

D
De la Porte, Caroline 31, 33
De Moll, Frederick 81, 126, 150
Denmark 5, 11, 19, 23, 26, 30ff, 36, 39–42, 47ff, 52ff, 59f, 65–68, 73f, 76f, 81ff, 100–105, 111, 113f, 119, 123, 126f, 149
digital education 45f, 70, 72, 94, 98, 100, 113, 120
Duignan, Maresa 149

E

Early Childhood Pedagogy Professional 66, 86f, 90, 93, 95, 98, 102
ECEC counsellors 11, 47, 76–80, 31
ECEC service providers 14, 39f, 42, 47, 64f, 67f, 71, 76f, 79, 86, 109f, 112, 114ff, 130ff, 147
ECEC system types 19–22, 42, 80, 86, 93
Engels-Kritidis, Rozalina 97ff, 149
England 5, 20, 26ff, 39ff, 43, 47, 52, 126
Estonia 5, 11, 19, 23, 30ff, 36, 39, 42, 45, 47f, 50, 52ff, 59f, 65f, 73f, 76, 81ff, 86, 105, 111, 119ff, 123f, 149
European Education and Culture Executive Agency (EACEA) 12, 19, 33, 42, 111
European Commission 12, 19, 33, 41f, 46, 111, 123, 134
European Credit Transfer and Accumulation System (ECTS) 69, 89, 93ff, 98f, 101ff, 113, 115, 132, 152
European Qualifications Framework (EQF) 29, 83, 90, 106, 120, 124, 152
European Quality Framework for ECEC 46
European Union 5, 11
Eurydice 12, 19, 33, 42, 51, 111
evaluation 24, 26, 46–50, 68, 70ff, 76, 89, 95, 119, 127, 130

F

field practice 13, 71, 94ff, 99f, 100–103, 114, 119, 122, 131, 133
Fielding, Michael 85
Finland 5, 11, 19f, 24, 31f, 37–42, 47f, 51f, 55, 59f, 65f, 68f, 73f, 77, 81f, 86, 93, 100–103, 106, 115, 121, 124, 149
France 5, 11, 21f, 25, 28, 35, 37f, 41, 44, 46ff, 50, 52f, 55, 62f, 65ff, 69, 75, 78f, 100, 103, 106f, 112, 116, 121, 124, 125, 127, 149
Fuchs-Rechlin, Kirsten 77

G

Garvis, Susanne 67
German Federal Ministry for Family Affairs, Senior Citizens, Women and Youth 5, 11, 147
Germany 5, 11f, 20f, 24, 26, 31, 33, 36, 39ff, 43, 45, 48f, 52, 54f, 59, 61, 64–68, 74, 77, 79, 81, 83, 86, 88, 101, 105, 107, 109, 111, 113ff, 122, 149
Greece 5, 11, 21f, 25, 28, 35, 37f, 40, 44, 46–50, 52, 54, 59, 63, 66–69, 75, 78f, 86, 101f, 107, 114, 116, 123, 125, 127, 149
Gulbrandsen, Lars 87, 124, 150
Gwinner, Anne 139

H

Hadjar, Andreas 150
Harring, Dana 139
Heikka, Johanna 67
Hostettler Schärer, Janine 150
Hujala, Eeva 67
Hungary 5, 11, 21f, 35–38, 40f, 44, 46ff, 50, 52f, 55, 63–66, 69, 75, 78, 86, 90f, 100f, 105, 107, 112, 116, 123, 125, 149

I

Iannone, Rosa Lisa 109
Infant-Toddler Professional 66
inclusion 24f, 80ff, 97, 100, 120, 127, 134

induction measures 113, 115, 116, 122, 132
initial professional education (IPE) 11, 13, 60, 85f, 88, 92f, 95, 100f, 103ff, 119f, 131ff
IPE competence profiles 85–92
IPE curricula 93–100
IPE practicum (see field practice)
Ireland 5, 11, 21f, 25, 28, 35, 39, 41, 44, 46ff, 53ff, 62f, 65f, 68, 75, 78, 82, 84, 116, 121, 123, 149
Italy 5, 11, 60f, 27, 29, 31, 33, 36, 39, 41, 43, 48, 50–53, 55, 61f, 64, 66, 71, 74, 77, 79, 83, 86, 88ff, 100–103, 105, 111, 114f, 122ff, 126f, 149

J
Jager, Jerneja 81, 87, 112, 150
Jensen, Bente 109
Jensen, Charlotte Riis 113
Jensen, Jytte Juul 68, 119, 149

K
Kagan, Sharon Lynn 17
Kaiser, Anna-Katharina 77
Karlsson Lohmander, Maelis 81, 94f, 102, 109, 115, 124, 150
Kemp, Valérie 150
kindergarten/s 24ff, 28ff, 37, 40f, 46, 48, 50ff, 55, 60f, 64f, 67ff, 72ff, 78f, 81, 88, 90, 97f, 110, 119f, 122
Kindergarten Educator 29, 120, 125
Kindergarten Teacher 65, 69, 83, 86, 102
Kirsch, Claudine 150
Klinkhammer, Nicole 46
Koch, Anette 68, 119, 149
Korintus, Marta 64, 91, 149
Krenn-Wache, Marisa 95f, 120, 149

L

Larsen, Trine P. 31, 33
Latvia 5, 11, 19, 26, 31f, 36ff, 42, 47ff, 53, 59f, 64, 66, 73f, 77, 81, 100, 103, 111, 113, 115, 121, 123, 126, 149
leadership 24, 26, 67ff, 72, 85, 102f, 113, 127
legal entitlement to a place in ECEC, 25f, 31ff, 35f, 55
Lipnická, Milena 150
Lithuania 5, 11, 19f, 24, 33, 36ff, 40ff, 47, 49f, 52–55, 59, 61, 64ff, 68, 73f, 76, 81ff, 100, 103, 106, 111, 115, 121, 123, 126f, 149
Liukineviciene, Laima 68
Loizou, Eleni 81, 149
Loudová Stralczynská, Barbora 64, 122, 149
Lumsden, Eunice 82, 150
Lunneblad, Johannes 67
Luxembourg 5, 11, 20f, 24, 33, 36ff, 41, 43f, 47–55, 62, 66, 68, 74, 77, 81, 83, 106, 111, 115, 125f, 150
Lynch, Zuzana 150

M
MacDonald, Natalie 150
Malta 5, 11, 20f, 24, 29, 31f, 34, 36, 39ff, 43, 48f, 52, 54, 61f, 64–69, 74, 77, 81, 83, 86, 101, 106, 109, 114f, 120 ,123ff, 127, 150
Maniates, Helen 68
Matković, Teo 111
Miňová, Monika 112f, 150
Miskeljin, Lidija 81, 96f, 150
Mitchell, Linda 54
Moss, Peter 17, 54, 85
multi-age ECEC settings 40, 41, 151

N
The Netherlands 5, 11, 21f, 25, 28, 36f, 39, 44, 47ff, 52, 63, 65ff, 75,

155

78f, 86, 90f, 101 ,106f, 114, 125, 127, 150
newly qualified staff 113, 115, 122, 133
Nicholson, Julie 67f
Northern Ireland 20. 27, 32, 43ff, 83
Norway 5, 19, 24, 28, 31, 33, 39f, 43, 43, 48f, 51–54, 59, 61, 65ff, 73f, 76, 81ff, 86f, 100, 103, 109, 111, 115, 120, 124, 150
Nóvoa, Antonio 17, 129
nurseries 40, 59, 64, 77, 90, 119

O

Oberhuemer, Pamela 11f, 19, 21f, 33, 35f, 38, 43f, 53, 61f, 64, 74f, 77, 89, 102, 104, 113f, 122, 147, 149
O'Sullivan, June 67

P

Pacholczyk-Sanfilippo, Marta 150
parenting leave 32, 53ff, 130
part-integrated ECEC system 20f, 24, 26, 33, 41, 43, 45, 55, 59, 61, 65, 74, 77, 79, 81, 83, 88, 95, 109, 111, 115, 129f, 151
Peleman, Brecht 149
Peterson, Tiina 81, 121, 149
Petrescu, Anca 150
Picchio, Mariacristina 78, 89, 103, 122, 126, 149
Pirard, Florence 114, 120, 149
Pre-primary and Primary Education Professional 88, 102
Pre-primary Education Professional 66, 95
probationary period 115f
Poland 5, 11, 21f, 30, 32, 36ff, 44, 47–52, 54, 55, 62f, 75, 78f, 100ff, 105, 110, 112, 116, 120, 126f, 150

Portugal 5, 11, 21f, 25, 36, 39f, 44, 46–54, 62f, 66, 75, 78, 82, 93, 97–100, 103, 105, 116, 123ff, 127, 129, 150
Preus, Marianne 113

Q

qualification requirements 11, 20f, 60–63, 67, 69, 74f, 79f, 82, 87, 93, 96, 98, 106, 120, 129, 131

R

Rayna, Sylyie 37, 149
Reinertz, Catherine 149
Rogers, Catriona 150
Romania 5, 11, 20f, 25, 27, 30, 34, 37f, 43, 47f, 51, 53, 55, 62, 64, 66, 74, 77, 79, 81, 83, 100, 103, 105, 109, 111, 115, 123f, 150
Romijn, Bodine 91f, 150
Roth, Jessica L. 17
Russia 5, 12, 20f, 31f, 34, 39ff, 43, 48, 53ff, 60, 62, 64ff, 74, 77, 83, 86, 106, 115, 120, 123, 126f, 150

S

Sabaliauskas, Eigirsdas 81, 149
Sakellariou, Maria 149
Sakr, Mona 67
Schäfer, Britta 139
Scheiwe, Kirsten 36
Schreyer, Inge 11, 19, 21f, 33, 35f, 38, 43f, 53, 61f, 64, 74f, 77, 89, 102, 113f, 122, 147, 149
Scotland 20, 28, 43, 52, 83, 106, 115
Serbia 5, 20f, 27, 29, 32, 34, 37f, 40f, 43, 48, 50, 53ff, 62, 64ff, 68, 74, 77, 81, 83, 86, 93, 95ff, 100, 105, 111f, 115, 150
Sharmahd, Nima 109, 149
Siarova, Hanna 149
Simoes Loureiro, Kevin 150
Singer, Elly 91f, 150

Slovakia/Slovak Republic 5, 11, 21f, 26, 29, 36ff, 41, 44, 46–50, 52, 54f, 60, 63, 66f, 69, 75, 78f, 83, 111f, 114, 116, 120, 123, 126, 150

Slovenia 5, 11, 19, 28f, 31, 33, 39f, 43, 48ff, 52ff, 59, 61, 64–67, 69, 73f, 77, 81f, 86f, 106, 111f, 115, 120, 126, 150

Social and Childhood Pedagogy Professional 66, 88, 102

Social Care/Health Care Professional 66

Spring, Heidi Honig 113

Spring, Frank 113

Sofii, Nataliia 73, 80, 150

Sollars, Valerie 82, 150

Sousa, Diana 17

Spain 5, 11, 20f, 25, 27, 30, 34, 36, 39ff, 43, 47, 49, 51f, 54, 62, 64, 68ff, 74, 77, 81ff, 100ff, 115, 121ff, 125, 127, 150

student mentors 103

Šūpule, Inese 149

specialist support staff 13, 59, 71, 80f, 131

staff shortages 13, 106, 119–123, 133

Sweden 5, 11, 19f, 26, 31ff, 37–40, 42f, 47f, 53f, 59, 61, 64–69, 71, 73–77, 81ff, 86, 93ff, 100, 102f, 106, 109, 111, 115, 120, 123, 127, 150

Switzerland 5, 21f, 36ff, 44, 46, 52ff, 46–67, 69, 75, 78, 82, 100, 106, 112, 116, 124, 127, 150

T

teacher education/training (see initial professional education)

U

UK – see United Kingdom

Ukraine 5, 12, 19, 24, 26, 31, 33, 37–40, 43, 45, 48f, 52ff, 59, 59, 61, 65f, 69, 72ff, 76f, 80ff, 105, 111, 115, 119, 123, 150

Ulich, Mica 11

unitary ECEC system 19, 23, 26, 32, 39f, 42, 45, 55, 59f, 68, 73f, 76, 79f, 82f, 86, 88, 93, 109, 11f, 115, 125, 130f, 151

United Kingdom 5, 11, 31f, 34ff, 39, 43ff, 52, 54f, 65, 67, 74, 106, 110, 115, 126, 150

Urban, Mathias 85

V

van Laere, Katrin 149

Vandenbroeck. Michel 85

Veisson, Marika 81, 121, 149

Volkova, Tatiana 120, 150

W

Wales 20, 27, 40, 47, 83, 106, 120

Weßler-Poßberg, Dagmar 113

Willekens, Harry 36

Williams, Pia 120

Wysłowska, Olga 150

Z

Żytko, Małgorzata 110, 150

Elina Fonsén | Raisa Ahtiainen
Marja Heikkinen | Lauri Heikonen
Petra Strehmel | Emanuel Tamir (eds.)

Early Childhood Education Leadership in Times of Crisis

International Studies During the COVID-19

2023 • 264 pp. • Paperback • 39,90 € (D) • 41,10 € (A)
ISBN 978-3-8474-2683-7 • also available as e-book in open access

The COVID-19 pandemic has dramatically affected all aspects of professional and private life worldwide, including the field of early childhood education and care (ECE). This volume sheds light on leadership in ECE: How did leaders experience the challenges they were facing and what coping strategies did they apply in order to deal with the changes in everyday life and practices in ECE centres? Authors from twelve countries present empirical findings gaining information on different crisis management mechanisms in ECE systems around the world.

www.shop.budrich.de

Yves Schemeil

The Making of the World

How International Organizations Shape Our Future

2023 • 406 pp. • Paperback • 44,90 € (D) • 46,20 € (A)
ISBN 978-3-8474-2146-7 • also available as e-book in open access

International Organizations (IOs) were designed to provide global public goods, among which security for all, trade for the richest, and development for the poorest. Their very existence is now a promise of success for the cooperative turn in international relations. Although the IO network was once created by established powers, rising states can hardly resist the massive production of norms that their governments can be reluctant to respect without being able to discard them. IOs are omnipresent, and exert great influence on the world as we know it. However, rulers and ruled are hardly aware of such compelling and snowballing processes. Yves Schemeil uses his in-depth knowledge of IOs to analyze their current impact on international relations, on world politics, and their potential of shaping the global future.

www.shop.budrich.de

Simone Seitz
Petra Auer
Rosa Bellacicco (eds.)

International Perspectives on Inclusive Education

In the Light of Educational Justice

2023. 268 pp. • Paperback • 59,90 € (D) • 61,60 € (A)
ISBN 978-3-8474-2698-1 • also available as e-book in open access

International developments and impulses call for the equitable and inclusive design of education systems. This book takes this up and focuses on the often blurred relationship between inclusive education and educational equity. By compiling current research results and theoretical contributions from several European countries on the topic, the authors create an overarching framework for discussion.

www.shop.budrich.de